"The truth is, once I began reading this manuscript I could not put the book down! It is my view that Dr. Allan Botkin has made a major breakthrough in the treatment of those suffering from the emotional consequences of loss and grief."

—The Rev. Dr. Ralph S. Leonard, Vice President Emeritus for Church Relations, Carthage College, Kenosha, Wisconsin

"Dr. Botkin has hit upon a fascinating and powerful new tool that may not only help his clients cope with their losses, but also breaks new ground in understanding life and death."

—Bruce Greyson, M.D., Professor of Psychiatric Medicine, University of Virginia, School of Medicine; Editor, *Journal of Near-Death Studies*

"There have been very few major breakthroughs in the field of psychology in the last hundred years, and Dr. Allan Botkin has certainly achieved one of them. His discovery has implications that go well beyond clinical practice."

—Alan L. Strand, Ph.D., psychologist

"*Induced After-Death Communication: A New Therapy for Healing Grief and Trauma* is an authentic and believable story of Dr. Botkin's groundbreaking discovery of a new and very powerful treatment for grief. But even more than that, the book provides readers with a whole new way of thinking about and experiencing our relationships and our lives. The book offers hope and comfort, and a new kind of peace of mind.

"The book is written in a compelling style that makes it difficult to put down and leaves you hungry for more. This is not only a book for psychologists and psychotherapists, but for all people who seek to understand the meaning of life, and death.

—Linda Harper, Ph.D., psychologist, author

INDUCED
AFTER
DEATH
COMMUNICATION

A New Therapy
for Healing Grief and Trauma

ALLAN L. BOTKIN, PSY.D.

WITH R. CRAIG HOGAN, PH.D.

HAMPTON ROADS
PUBLISHING COMPANY, INC.

Cover design by Marjoram Productions
Cover art © Loyd Chapplow. All rights reserved.

Hampton Roads Publishing Company, Inc.
1125 Stoney Ridge Road
Charlottesville, VA 22902

434-296-2772
fax: 434-296-5096
e-mail: hrpc@hrpub.com
www.hrpub.com

If you are unable to order this book from your local
bookseller, you may order directly from the publisher.
Call 1-800-766-8009, toll-free.

Library of Congress Cataloging-in-Publication Data

Botkin, Allan L.
  Induced after-death communication : a new therapy for healing grief and trauma /
Allan L. Botkin with R. Craig Hogan.
      p. cm.
  Summary: "Relates the story of how Dr. Botkin, while using a variation of EMDR
therapy, discovered a new therapy for helping patients permanently overcome grief
and trauma. Dr. Botkin used this therapy primarily with Vietnam War veterans in his
work at a VA hospital"--Provided by publisher.
  Includes bibliographical references (p.).
  ISBN 1-57174-423-1 (6x9 tp : alk. paper)
  1. Grief therapy. 2. Psychic trauma--Treatment. 3. Post-traumatic stress
disorder--Treatment. 4. Eye movement desensitization and reprocessing. 5.
Spiritualism. I. Hogan, R. Craig. II. Title.
  RC455.4.L67B68 2005
  616.89'14--dc22
                              2005013232

ISBN 1-57174-423-1
10 9 8 7 6 5 4 3 2 1
Printed on acid-free paper in the United States

Contents

Acknowledgments

First and foremost, I am forever indebted to the combat veterans I worked with as a psychologist for over 20 years in a Veterans Administration (VA) hospital. They served in WWII, Korea, Vietnam, Desert Storm, and a variety of other dangerous situations. I learned to admire and respect these veterans, not only for their courage in combat, but also for their courage in confronting their deepest pain in therapy. The discovery presented in this book was shared in the most intimate way with these veterans. At times we cried, and at other times we laughed until it hurt. We hugged often. I miss those guys. Since retiring from the VA, I go back and visit them from time to time. We were, and still are, like family.

This book would not have been possible if it weren't for those pioneers who laid the foundation for the ideas it contains. Although I never met Dr. Elisabeth Kubler-Ross (she passed away in 2004), she did more than any other human being to establish death and dying as legitimate professional and scientific subjects. I also express my deeply held appreciation for Dr. Francine Shapiro who provided us with the most powerful psychological technique ever known to alleviate human suffering.

In my journey, I have been honored to receive encouragement and support from a few of my heroes and leaders in the field: Dr. Raymond Moody, Dr. Bruce Greyson, and Bill Guggenheim. Each is well known worldwide, and each has made significant contributions to the field either of near-death experiences or after-death communications. Although I have had the opportunity to meet and discuss my findings with Raymond and Bill, I have yet to meet in person Dr. Greyson, who consistently stepped in by phone and mail to provide timely professional support when I desperately needed it. Thank you, Dr. Greyson.

You would not be reading this book right now if Frank Demarco, the cofounder and editor in chief of Hampton Roads Publishing Company, did not save this manuscript, at the last minute, from going into the trash bin. Getting published has been a long, and at times, very frustrating endeavor. More than anything, I want Frank, at some point, to feel that he made the right decision in backing this work.

As a psychologist, I never envisioned myself writing a book for the general public. Although I had published a few scientific papers, I realized that my writing skills were very limited and that I couldn't do it on my own. I needed a good professional writer, preferably one who had a personal and intellectual appreciation for this discovery. Finding the right writer has also not been easy. *Induced After-Death Communication* began to take on its current form only after Dr. Craig Hogan stepped in and helped me turn this discovery into a fun, readable book.

I also want to express my appreciation to Sheila Chapman, who is the coauthor for the screenplay version of this book. Her rapid, keen grasp of the concepts in this book and her ability to translate them into a moving and heartfelt screenplay have been awe-inspiring. Her professional writing skills have also done much to improve the overall quality of the presentation of the discovery presented in this book.

I want to offer a special thanks to Professor Ralph Leonard, a remarkable individual with extensive academic training and experience in theology and grief counseling, for his ongoing and enthusiastic support of this work.

From time to time, I think about colleagues who provided support and encouragement along the way. I want to express my gratitude to Karen Paddock, Dr. Sheilah Perrin, Greg Rimoldi, Dr. David Mannelli, Dr. Kathy Parker, Dr. Merle Moffat, Dr. John Schaut, Dr. Howard Lipke, Dr. Ivan Aubuchon, Dr. Mitch Goodman, Dr. Stacey Jones, Dr. Kimberly Kroll, Dr. Jo-Ann Nishimoto, Dr. Alan Strand, Dr. Carol Paxton-Cox, and Dr. Darcy Mouton.

A number of professionals across the United States have now received formal IADC training and are in on the ground floor of IADC. They include Katelyn Daniels (IL), Dr. Karen Sherman (NY), Dr. Susan Becker (FL), Pati Zimmerman (OR), Hania Stromberg (NM), Becky Morris (PA), Tina Bramson (IL), Dr. Linda Harper (IL), Dr. Don Dufford (CA), and Dr. Jan Holden (TX). This list will continue to grow and, it is to be hoped, at some point there will be trained IADC therapists available for all people interested in the IADC experience.

Dr. Holden is a professor at the University of North Texas who plans to conduct research projects on IADC with her graduate students. Her work will do much to further our understanding of IADCs.

Along the way, I chanced upon loyal supporters who always seemed to be there when I needed them for help in promoting this discovery. I want to give a heartfelt thanks to Diane Willis, coordinator of the Chicago International Association for Near-Death Studies (IANDS), and to "Bobby," a loyal supporter who has done much to get this information out to the public.

Last, and certainly not least, I thank my family for being there for me all along, and especially during the last few years of risk and uncertainty in my endeavor. My parents, Edith and Leroy Botkin, never let up on their abundance of unconditional love and support. All my love to Barbara, Allie, and Max, who, more than anyone else, had to put up with me during this book-writing phase—thanks for loving me back.

Foreword

Life after death is not yet a scientific issue, but experiences suggestive of an afterlife have been an important clinical issue for some time. It is well known, for example, that patients who are resuscitated after close calls with death often have inspiring tales of afterlife adventures to tell. So, doctors involved in the care of these patients need to be able to listen sympathetically. The survivors of close calls need to be reassured that they are not alone and that several medical studies show that an appreciable percentage of those who return from death's door tell of leaving their bodies and entering into a bright, comforting light of love. These patients also tell of reunions with loved ones lost to death during these life-changing out-of-body interludes.

Seeing apparitions of loved ones lost to death, or feeling their presence vividly, is also a surprisingly common experience. So, again, clinicians need to be able to discuss these experiences with patients, who sometimes need counseling to help them integrate such profound spiritual experiences into their everyday lives.

Anyone who works with patients in the throes of grief knows how common apparitions of the deceased are. Grief counselors are also generally aware that these apparitional encounters greatly promote the healing process. Grief counselors will attest to how often grieving patients say, "If I only had five more minutes."

The work Dr. Allan Botkin reports in this book takes clinical work with grieving patients to an entirely new level. He reports on his development of a fascinating clinical method for giving people exactly that—five more minutes to say the goodbyes and I love you and other things left unsaid, and to tidy up unfinished business. I will leave it to him to describe his method and results, which he does very thoroughly in this riveting book.

Incredible as it may seem, there is a long history of documented techniques that elicit experiences of the deceased. The ancient Greeks engaged in such practice and it was continued by medical doctors in Europe well into the Middle Ages. So, although Dr. Botkin's work may raise some eyebrows in twenty-first century America, it is actually just the latest wrinkle in a human tradition that goes back to prehistory. Indeed, we can even say that evocation of the deceased is part of the collective cultural heritage of humankind.

In Ancient Greece, evocation of spirits was practiced in subterranean institutions known as psychomanteums or, as it is often translated, oracles of the dead. These places were built entirely beneath the earth, with the darkness providing ideal conditions of sensory deprivation. By reading ancient Greek texts and combining what I read there with my psychiatric knowledge of grief counseling, I developed a method of preparing subjects for this experience. Basically, it consists simply of getting them to talk and reminisce about a departed loved one they wish to see again. After they bring up their memories of the deceased, they sit in the apparition chamber, relax and gaze into a mirror in a dimly lit room.

Under those circumstances, about half or more of the subjects have vivid, lifelike encounters with the spirits of the deceased. They see their loved ones in three dimensions, full color, and seeming vibrantly alive. About one-third of the subjects who have experiences report hearing the audible voice of the deceased.

Almost all the rest say that although they heard no audible voice, they had an experience of heart-to-heart communications during which they felt they were in contact with the departed. Most importantly, these subjects say that they feel their experiences brought them closer to resolution of their grief.

Subsequent to my work, other psychologists have re-created my procedure and achieved identical results. All of us who have worked with it agree that the method holds promise as a technique for helping people with grief.

Dr. Allan Botkin has developed a different and very powerful psychological procedure for evoking experiences of the deceased. I was fascinated when I fist heard him describe it as I am sure you will be, too.

To his credit, Dr. Botkin does not present his work as "scientific evidence of life after death." He and I agree that it is too early for science to tackle the biggest of the big questions of existence and humankind's ultimate mystery. Instead, he is content to put his findings forward in hopes that they may be of clinical benefit to those who have lost loved ones and who are struggling with grief. For this, I commend him and hope that his exciting new method will inspire new research. And I believe that his readers will get as much enjoyment and stimulation from his book as I have.

Raymond A. Moody, Jr., Ph.D., M.D.

Notes

The Cases

The cases presented in this book are all real. They occurred in therapists' offices or, in the case of after-death communications that happened unexpectedly and spontaneously, were reported to the therapists by patients. All details that might identify patients have been changed to protect patient confidentiality. To protect confidentiality further, we occasionally combine two cases that are similar. In all instances, the substance and the results are what actually occurred.

IADC

The abbreviation "IADC" is a registered trademark owned by Allan L. Botkin, Psy.D., and stands for "induced after-death communication."

Note on EMDR

In IADC therapy, eye movement desensitization and reprocessing (EMDR) is used in a way that differs significantly from the way it is presented in standard EMDR training. The research that supports the use of EMDR, therefore, does not necessarily support the method of using EMDR described in this book.

Preface

Nothing in my formal training in psychology prepared me for the events described in this book. After years of treating the victims of psychological trauma, I began to experiment with a relatively new and very powerful treatment called eye movement desensitization and reprocessing, or EMDR. What I discovered appeared to defy everything we knew about treating patients suffering from grief and trauma, and it took me into a realm of human experience unfamiliar to me.

I discovered a way of helping ordinary, everyday people have an after-death communication experience that resolves feelings of grief resulting from a death to a degree that was not considered possible in the field of grief therapy. A group of psychotherapists and I have induced the experience with several thousand patients and people wanting to experience a reconnection with a lost loved one. It is a consistently positive, loving experience most people are able to have while sitting in a trained psychotherapist's office.

I am Allan L. Botkin, Psy.D., a psychologist with 20 years' experience working with thousands of patients at a Chicago Veterans Administration hospital and in my private practice, the Center for Grief and Traumatic Loss in Libertyville, Illinois. My coauthor is R. Craig Hogan, Ph.D., formerly a professor of business communications at three universities, professor and interpersonal development coordinator in the graduate school at

Wheaton College in Wheaton, Illinois, curriculum specialist at a medical school, and author of "The Personal Styles Inventory" as well as articles and books to help people improve their interpersonal work relationships. In recent years, Dr. Hogan has devoted himself to studying and writing about consciousness, the nature of reality, and after-death communication. His interest in the latter was further piqued when I performed on him the procedure described in this book and he had two after-death communication experiences.

This book is told from my point of view because it describes what I discovered in my therapy practice. Know, however, that Dr. Hogan's thoughts are intertwined with mine as we tell this remarkable story together, though we use "I" and "me" pronouns.

The after-death communication induction requires use of EMDR, a powerful psychotherapeutic procedure that can be applied only by a licensed psychotherapist with EMDR training. Hence, nonprofessionals cannot induce after-death communication in themselves or induce it in others. The healing, uplifting experience is, however, available to anyone who contacts a trained psychotherapist to have the procedure done. Information about therapists available to perform the procedure and about training for therapists is available at our Web site, http://inducedadc.com. For an explanation of the procedure an EMDR-trained psychotherapist can use to induce the experience, see appendix B of this book.

The therapy method has worked for nearly everyone with whom we have had sessions. I and several dozen other psychotherapists have induced well over three thousand of the experiences with people from a wide range of professional, experiential, and religious backgrounds. We now know that a patient's beliefs have no effect on the outcome. It works equally well for the devoutly religious, the highly spiritual, agnostics, and atheists. It works for patients experiencing normal bereavement and those suffering from horrendous traumatic grief. It works for patients with recent losses as well as for those who have suffered a loss many decades in the past. In short, it appears to work with nearly everyone, nearly all of the time.

The person experiences a healing from within. The psychologist often sits in silence watching for long periods while the person, quietly, with eyes closed, has an experience that profoundly reduces feelings of guilt, anger, and sadness over a loved one's death. Afterward most experiencers assert with conviction that they had an after-death communication experience that changed their feelings of guilt, anger, and sadness to contentment, happiness, and a sense the lost loved one is well.

This book presents the story of the discovery of this therapeutic method, case studies of people who have been healed by it, and the procedure used to induce the psychological state necessary for the experience to occur.

The book includes a large number of combat-veteran cases. The reason is that I was a psychotherapist on a post-traumatic stress disorder unit at a Veterans Administration hospital for 20 years. I simply had a large number of veterans working through traumatic memories and feelings of loss from their experiences in combat who had the after-death communication experience. I have found, however, that the approach to therapy and the resulting after-death communication experiences are identical to those of civilian cases.

While some readers will embrace the discovery in this book easily because it is consistent with what they already believe to be true, others will read it with a healthy degree of skepticism. I was trained as a behavioral psychologist with a research background, so I will never lose my scientist's skepticism. I would not be presenting this if I did not feel, wholeheartedly, that the therapy method has worth and should be explored by the psychotherapeutic community. I simply ask that you resist allowing your skepticism about these phenomena to close down your openness to hearing about this therapy that works, and does so dramatically. It doesn't matter what I believe or the patient believes or you believe. IADC therapy appears to heal grief regardless of beliefs.

What I discovered is consistent with the direction in which the field of grief therapy started to turn prior to the IADC discovery. It asserts that, rather than disengage from the deceased, those in grief should continue a changing, dynamic relationship with the loved one. This new direction is already starting to take hold. I hope that IADC therapy contributes to the growth of that movement.

This discovery has deepened my understanding of life, of people, and of my profession. I hope it does the same for you.

1

An After-Death Communication Occurs Unexpectedly during Therapy

The beginning of knowledge is the discovery of something we
do not understand.

—Frank Herbert

Becky excitedly described to me what she experienced. "I saw my mother," she said, a broad smile across her tear-stained face. "I told her, 'I love you,' and she said, 'I love you too.' Then she hugged me. I could actually feel her arms around me."

But at the time of this experience, Becky's mother had been dead for five years.

Becky wasn't describing a dream. She was sitting in my office when she had the experience. She said she felt the touch of her mother's arms and was joyful to see her mother's smiling face, but only she and I were there and her eyes were closed. Her mother's warm, familiar embrace seemed vibrant and alive, but her mother was dead.

Her sense that she felt the touch of her deceased mother's arms was unusual enough, but the life change that resulted was remarkable. "I've been an atheist my whole life," she said, "but I'm sure now there really is a life after death. I used to worry about dying, and I felt so much pain when my mother died. I know now, though, that my fear and grief were based on something I didn't understand. I know that everything is OK and that I need to remember this when I feel life is getting me down." Her grief reduced dramatically and remained resolved in the months that followed.

When Becky came to my office that day for help to alleviate the deep sadness she was feeling over her mother's death, I was able to use a new form of therapy I had discovered to help reduce her grief. The method was available to me because I had learned how to use it through a long journey that began with a session in which it occurred by accident and progressed through identifying how I could help a patient experience it at will.

The story of that discovery follows.

My Skeptical Behavioral Scientist Training

The radical behaviorist movement was at its peak in the 1960s and was nowhere stronger than among a group of professors at the University of Kansas in Lawrence, where I was an undergraduate psychology major. Radical behaviorism asserted that only observable behaviors are worthy of scientific consideration. The practice of inferring private, mental events in people may be appropriate for mind readers and other nonscientific thinkers, but it had no place in a science of psychology. We were confident that inferences about inner states are unnecessary because understanding the relationship between observable behaviors and environmental variables is all that is needed to understand people's problems and provide treatment.

I carried that behaviorist, scientific underpinning into my master's degree studies at Illinois State University and through my work in community mental health for three years. I became adept at counting behaviors while manipulating the environment to evaluate how the counts changed. Finally, I ended my formal studies at Baylor University in Waco, Texas, in the comfortable familiarity of a cognitive-behavioral paradigm, the most widely accepted scientific psychological model of the early 1980s that continues to dominate psychology today.

No matter how my perspectives broaden, the instincts and skepticism of the scientist will never leave me. Anything I believe must be verifiable.

After completing my Doctor of Psychology (Psy.D.) at Baylor, I accepted a position at a Chicago-area Veterans Administration hospital working with post-traumatic stress disorder veterans, a focus that was to become my career. The first seven or eight years of using the cognitive-behavioral model with these traumatized vets were grueling for me and for my patients. The half-dozen professional staff on the unit all felt the same. The prevailing cognitive-behavioral model for treating victims of psychological trauma was "exposure therapy." We repeatedly exposed patients to reminders of their traumatic experiences in a safe, supportive environment so that, over time, their intense emotional responses might decrease in intensity.

While the approach made sense from a theoretical point of view, and we did get some modest results, the therapeutic changes were minimal and didn't appear to hold up over time.

A New Technique Dramatically Reduces Trauma and Grief

Then, in the late 1980s, psychologist Francine Shapiro, Ph.D., discovered a radical new therapy technique she named eye movement desensitization and reprocessing, or EMDR. In EMDR therapy, the psychotherapist, usually sitting before and slightly to the side of the patient, moves his or her hand, with the index and next finger extended, left and right in front of the patient on the same level as the patient's eyes. While focusing on the psychotherapist's hand and keeping the head stationary, so only the eyes move left and right rhythmically, the patient attends to a disturbing thought, feeling, sensation, or image.

During a set of eye movements, the patient experiences a spontaneous, natural reprocessing of the thought, feeling, sensation, or image. After a number of sets of eye movements, patients typically report psychological breakthroughs that normally would take months to achieve. The procedure is now being used for a wide variety of disorders, from multiple personality disorder to the post-traumatic stress disorders I worked with.

Experience has taught me that EMDR does two things better than any other approach. First, it rapidly and completely uncovers past traumatic events that are repressed or partially remembered. It is very common for a patient to say something like, "I can see the whole thing very clearly now" or "I felt like I was back there again." This experience by itself does very little to help the patient resolve the traumatic experience and, in fact, patients generally feel very distressed when they fully uncover a traumatic memory.

Once the traumatic memory is fully accessed in this way, however, the second strength of EMDR is that it allows the patient to process the memory so that the reliving component of the memory is eliminated, and the patient can then remember the traumatic event in a more abstract way. It is clear that this processing can only occur if the traumatic event is first uncovered and fully accessed.

No one is quite sure how it works, although it is apparent that it speeds up mental processing and is similar to the rapid eye movements (REMs) people experience in dream sleep. It is well known that during dream sleep, our brains process information at a higher rate than when we are awake. It has been assumed that this increased processing during sleep causes the rapid, back-and-forth eye movement. Having a fully awake person purposefully shift the eyes in the same way, as in EMDR, seems to cause the brain to process information more rapidly and efficiently. Thus EMDR draws upon the person's own natural ability to heal.

A number of studies have looked at the effects of EMDR on brain functioning. Levin, Lazrove, and van der Kolk (1999), for example, used neuroimaging to study the effects of EMDR. It was found that when subjects accessed a traumatic memory prior to EMDR, deep structures in the brain that represent the sensory and emotional components of the traumatic event were activated in isolation. After EMDR treatment, however, areas of the brain that hold the memory in a more abstract or symbolic manner were also activated. These findings support the consistent clinical observation that prior to EMDR, when people access a traumatic memory, they feel they are reexperiencing the event; after EMDR, they are able to remember the event in a more abstract and emotionally detached manner. I know of no other psychotherapeutic technique that can demonstrate such a clear change in brain function and an accompanying dramatic shift in perspective reported by the patient.

EMDR Is Not Hypnosis

I am frequently asked if EMDR is similar to hypnosis. Professionals trained in both EMDR and hypnosis, including me, believe that the techniques involve two very different types of mental processing. The best way to explain the differences is to use this analogy. Consciousness is like an internal movie projector that ceaselessly projects mental images onto the mind's screen. Hypnosis gets a person into a relaxed, focused state so the projector slows down. Because the projector is slowed, hypnosis can be used to go back to places on the film where forgotten or repressed memories are thought to exist. While hypnosis can assist in retrieving memories, the problem is that a person in a hypnotic state is also very suggestible and may unknowingly put an event on the screen that in reality never occurred. False memories, as they are now called, can seem very real to the person after the hypnosis.

EMDR, on the other hand, accelerates information processing in the brain so it speeds up the consciousness projector. When people suffer from repeatedly experiencing a traumatic memory, their projectors are, in essence, stuck in time and keep replaying the moments when the event occurred. EMDR speeds up the projector, unsticking it to allow it to run smoothly. The traumatic event then ceases to intrude in an unwanted way into consciousness.

At the same time, EMDR does not increase the suggestibility of the subject, so false memories are not a problem with EMDR. In fact, I have used EMDR to undo false memories. Tim, for example, had an alcoholic mother who was prone to fits of rage. For years, he was very troubled by a vague memory of feeling smothered and having difficulty breathing in his mother's presence. While under hypnosis with another therapist, he developed an image in which his mother was holding a pillow over his face with the clear intent of trying to kill him.

When I used EMDR with Tim, he immediately went back to the time he felt smothered and clearly remembered that his mother was preparing to take him outside on a very cold day and was bundling him up in his snowsuit as he lay in his stroller. His mother had tied a scarf tightly around his face, which caused him to have some difficulty breathing. Without any suggestion from me, Tim discovered what really happened and, from that moment on, was no longer distressed by the memory. Had he discovered that his mother was trying to kill him, more EMDR would have been required to get his "stuck projector" running smoothly again.

EMDR Has Begun to Make Its Way into Mainstream Practice

EMDR is rapidly making its way into mainstream mental health. Over 30,000 professionals have been trained in EMDR therapy worldwide, and the number is growing. EMDR training is only available to people who are already recognized by their state as independent providers of mental health services.

To date, there have been 18 scientifically controlled studies of the efficacy of EMDR. Overall, these studies support the value of EMDR. In addition to reducing post-traumatic stress disorder problems, it is also effective in the treatment of grief, phobic and panic disorders, sexual dysfunction, dissociative disorders, performance difficulties, and chronic pain. EMDR is still in its infancy and other applications will certainly be found.

The weight of evidence for its effectiveness has prompted official endorsements of EMDR by the American Psychological Association Division 12: Clinical Psychology (1998), International Society for Traumatic Stress Studies (2000), Northern Ireland Department of Health (2001), United Kingdom Department of Health (2001), Israeli National Council for National Health (2002), and U.S. Veterans Administration/ Department of Defense (2004).

The most important testimony for the effectiveness of EMDR, however, is that we have seen it work repeatedly and reliably with thousands of our patients.

A Near Tragedy Teaches Me about EMDR Firsthand

A colleague and I on the post-traumatic stress disorder unit were preparing to complete the formal certification training at Dr. Francine Shapiro's EMDR Institute in Watsonville, California, when a very distressing event forced me to experience the power of EMDR before my training. My two-year-old son nearly asphyxiated when a piece of food lodged in his throat. He first began choking and we weren't sure what was happening; then he stopped breathing and started turning blue. A successful Heimlich maneuver dislodged the food and he survived the ordeal, but the image of my son, blue, frantic, and dying before my eyes became an intrusive image that disturbed me often for two weeks after the incident.

When I explained my distress to the colleague who was planning to go through EMDR training with me, he suggested he use the technique as we understood it then to help my mind reprocess the troubling memory. We did several sets of eye movements while I focused on the incident. In ten minutes, the image had lost its distressing nature for me, and my anxiety over it had decreased dramatically. It seemed too good to be true. The effect appeared to be due to my own inner processing of the memory, a source of healing I had learned in my behaviorist training as being inconsequential. But that was only the first rock to dislodge from the foundation of certainty about behaviorism I had stood upon since my earliest days at the University of Kansas.

We Begin Using EMDR Therapy with Remarkable Results

My colleague and I completed the EMDR training and began using it in our post-traumatic stress disorder unit at the Veterans Administration (VA) hospital to see the effects it would have on our unique patients. The results were dramatic. Often we achieved in a single session changes in patients that we had not been able to approximate after years of conventional psychotherapy. It was a heady time for us. Regularly, one of us could be seen scurrying down the hall into a colleague's office to excitedly describe a successful session with a patient, doing a high five in triumph.

In 1992, Dr. H. Lipke and I published "Case studies of eye movement desensitization and reprocessing (EMDR) with chronic post-traumatic stress disorder" in *Psychotherapy*. We were elated for our patients and for ourselves as professionals earnestly seeking ways to make a difference in our patients' lives.

EMDR proved especially powerful in healing grief. People who experience grief, especially traumatic grief, generally feel a variety of intense emotions. Initially, survivors often experience shock and numbing. Then, more chronic feelings of anger, guilt, and sadness surface; they may be crying one moment and full of anger or rage the next. A primary task for the psychotherapist is to create a supportive psychological environment in which patients can openly express these feelings and work through them.

By working through these feelings, patients are usually able to eventually achieve some level of acceptance of their loss and improved ability to get on with their lives. Generally, the loss is never fully resolved; reminders of the loss can trigger periods of sadness, guilt, or anger throughout the patient's life. Over time, however, these episodes usually decrease somewhat in frequency and intensity.

If, for example, parents have a child who is hit and killed by a car while playing in the street, the parents will likely experience all three of these

7

emotions (sadness, guilt, anger) very intensely at different moments. At times, they will be enraged at the driver who killed their child; at other times, they will feel intense guilt for having allowed their child to play in the street or for not watching their child more closely. In their most despairing moments, they will feel the cold clutch of intense sadness at their loss and the painful feeling of disconnection from their child.

It is my belief that at the core of grief is profound sadness. The core sadness is so painful that the patient unconsciously but effectively shrouds it in guilt and regret and gets stuck on "What if?" questions. What if I could have prevented her death? What if I had been a more loving friend? Both the guilt and sadness are often avoided by anger or rage—at God, the doctors, the commanding officer, or anyone else available as a target. The doctors should have been more attentive. Our lieutenant had no business putting us in that dangerous position. However powerful they seem when acted out, the layers of guilt and anger are only defenses the patient's mind uses to keep from feeling the painful sadness at the core.

The grief therapy we had been practicing before we began using EMDR therapy sought to reduce the immobilizing pain of grief by helping our patients peel off the shrouds of anger to reveal the guilt, then peel off the layers of guilt to reveal the sadness, then talk out their sadness to help them work through it. That process took years of frustration and seemingly endless therapy appointments. With EMDR, we could help patients rapidly process through all of these layers, sometimes in a single session.

Core-Focused EMDR Accesses the Core Sadness

EMDR had proven to be such a reliable, effective procedure for uncovering and alleviating traumatic grief that I felt comfortable with encouraging patients more strongly to go to the core sadness immediately and stay with it. I was able to bypass the overlying guilt and anger that preoccupied normal therapy sessions for months or years and go directly into the sadness in one session. When we were able to process the core sadness fully, guilt and anger tended to vanish without even being directly addressed. It demonstrated that guilt and anger serve only to protect patients from experiencing the deep sadness. I also found that patients responded better when they closed their eyes briefly after a set of eye movements, so I instructed all patients to close their eyes. I termed my direct approach to the underlying sadness "core-focused EMDR." The results were very successful and occurred even more rapidly than with standard EMDR.

Denny's case is an example. Denny, a combat veteran, lost a good friend during an intense firefight in Vietnam. His friend had been in Vietnam only a short time and Denny had taken it upon himself to show him the ropes. During this firefight, his friend raised his head above the barricade from which they were firing, was shot in the temple, and died instantly.

Denny finished telling me the story in a rage. "If that damned lieutenant hadn't ordered us where we knew we shouldn't have been, he'd still be alive." He said he had told his friend repeatedly before this battle to keep his head down, and he felt very guilty, turning his anger on himself, because he hadn't warned him again before this firefight. "I could have saved him. Why didn't I tell him again?"

I asked him whether he felt any sadness about his friend's death and he said he did feel some, but "only to a small degree." When I started the core-focused EMDR, I ignored the guilt and anger, telling him to pay attention to the sadness. I did a set of EMDR eye movements and his sadness increased quickly. He began to sob. I stayed with the sadness, administering more sets of eye movements until the sadness was at a peak. He cried and shook his head. "Stay with that feeling," I told him and administered more eye movements.

Finally, with additional core-focused EMDR, his sadness began to decrease. After several more sets, I asked him, "How is your sadness now?"

"It's pretty well gone," he said, smiling weakly. "I feel much better about it."

"What about your anger and guilt feelings?" I asked.

He thought for a moment. "Gone," he said. "I just feel like it happened and there's nothing I could do about it. No one could have told him enough times to keep his head down. It wasn't my fault."

Once the core-focused EMDR had addressed Denny's sadness, the guilt and anger disappeared. They were no longer needed to conceal the deep sadness at the root of all the emotions.

EMDR Lets Us Make a Difference in Our Patients' Lives

EMDR had proven to be a wondrous gift to our patients and us, and core-focused EMDR was taking our patients to their core problem, healing it in even more dramatic fashion.

The years that followed were filled with accomplishment and victories. We honed our skills and, in partnership with our patients' inner resources, made a difference in their lives. Our inpatient unit was one of the first in the country to use EMDR consistently and successfully. It seemed that we had a vista from which we could survey the known psychological terrain with confidence and optimism.

Then one day, during an otherwise normal session with a patient, the core-focused EMDR took me and the patient into a realm I didn't know existed.

A Patient Has an After-Death Communication in My Office

On the day I first discovered the induced after-death communication (IADC) phenomenon, I was in a psychotherapy session with Sam. I handed him a box of Kleenex as tears trailed down his face, dropping from his chin to his shirt. I had worked with Sam, a 46-year-old patient at the VA Hospital, on other traumatic memories of his Vietnam War experience, but he had avoided bringing up this one because it was too painful.

While in Vietnam, he had developed a very close relationship with Le, a ten-year-old orphaned Vietnamese girl. She had made Sam's base camp her home after both of her parents were killed. She helped with daily chores on the base and in return was given food, shelter, and companionship. The other American soldiers watched out for her, but Sam and Le developed a special relationship. Le reminded Sam of his two younger sisters, helping him maintain a sense of his own humanity amid the dehumanizing brutality of war.

Each time Sam's unit returned from his patrols in the jungle, Le would pick him out of the group, run to him, and give him a hug. Other soldiers in Sam's unit became accustomed to seeing them together talking about their lives before they met. Le particularly enjoyed his stories about life in America. After several months, Sam decided to adopt Le and bring her home.

Orders came from headquarters, however, that all orphaned Vietnamese children on the base were to be sent to a Catholic orphanage in a distant village. Sam was devastated. A few days later, Sam, in tears, helped load Le and the other orphaned Vietnamese children onto a flatbed truck to take them to the orphanage.

Just as they got all of the children onto the truck, shots rang out and bullets zipped past the truck. Risking their lives, Sam and the other soldiers quickly pulled the children off the truck to the relative safety of the ground. The shooting stopped as quickly as it had started, and they began to put the children back onto the truck. Nearly all of the children were back on the truck when Sam realized he didn't see Le. He walked to the back of the truck and saw her lying face down with a spot of blood on her back. Sam rolled her over and was horrified to see that her front torso was blown open from a bullet that had entered her back. Sam sat on the ground, holding her lifeless body, and cried. Other soldiers eventually had to pull Sam away and take Le's body to bury her.

The incident was Sam's psychological undoing.

For the remainder of his tour in Vietnam, he numbed the pain of his profound loss with anger and rage, volunteering for dangerous patrols to kill any enemy he could find or be killed himself. After Vietnam, he returned to the States and fathered a daughter, but then avoided her for years because she triggered anger, guilt, deep sadness over Le's death, and gruesome images of Le's dead body. For nearly 28 years, Sam spent most of his days secluded in the basement of his home, separated physically and psychologically from his family.

To help him open up and work through the grief that was dominating his life, I decided to use core-focused EMDR. Sam sobbed quietly from the overwhelming pain of his grief. I asked him to focus on his sadness while I administered the first set of eye movements. As I expected, the sadness that had held him isolated in grief for 28 years increased notably. I gave him more sets of eye movements and his sadness began to decrease.

While tears ran down his face, I administered a final eye movement procedure and asked him to close his eyes. Neither of us was prepared for what happened next. The tears that had been flowing from his closed eyes suddenly stopped, and he smiled broadly. He giggled softly. When he opened his eyes, he was euphoric.

"When I closed my eyes, I saw Le as a beautiful woman with long black hair in a white gown surrounded by a radiant light. She seemed genuinely happier and more content than anyone I have ever known." Sam's tear-reddened face glowed. "She thanked me for taking care of her before she died. I said, 'I love you, Le,' and she said 'I love you too, Sam,' and she put her arms around me and embraced me. Then she faded away."

Sam was ecstatic and absolutely convinced that he had just communicated with Le. "I could actually feel her arms around me," he proclaimed.

As Sam's psychologist, I wasn't sure what to make of what he was telling me. I assumed that the agony of his grief had somehow produced a hallucination based on fantasy or wishful thinking. I had never witnessed or heard of such a response during psychotherapy.

After Sam left my office on that day, the image of his smile showing through his tears and his assertive statement that he felt he had communicated with Le played repeatedly in my mind. I sat in the quiet of my office trying to understand what had happened.

Sam experienced a grief hallucination, I thought. I had heard of these. But that wasn't sufficient to explain what I had witnessed. The creativity had been remarkable. I had not seen that spontaneous imagination in any patient and had never read about anything similar in the literature. If that was a hallucination, then his mind had miraculously created an experience that was completely healing. During my clinical rotations on wards with the chronic and severely mentally ill, no patient ever reported a hallucination that was so positive and healing.

Something in Sam flowered in an instant, without direction from me, reversed the sadness in which he was immersed, and brought him a notable feeling of release from intrusive images, anxiety, and depression that had consumed him for 28 years.

I left the VA hospital building that day still feeling puzzled by what had happened. I wondered whether I would ever in my professional career see such a remarkable scene again. Probably not, I thought. Sam's experience was one of those events a psychotherapist would see once in a professional lifetime and I could just file it away as a one-time aberration. But I also felt concern that if Sam had hallucinated, the intense stress of his traumatic memories had somehow compromised his ability to differentiate reality from fantasy. That worried me.

2

How I Learned to Induce
After-Death Communications

Our normal waking consciousness, rational consciousness as we call it, is but one special type of consciousness, whilst all about it, parted from it by the filmiest of screens, there lie potential forms of consciousness entirely different. . . . No account of the universe in its totality can be final which leaves these other forms of consciousness quite discarded. How to regard them is the question. . . . At any rate, they forbid a premature closing of our accounts with reality.

—William James

Sam's apparent hallucination was on my mind the next day as I met with other patients. I thought through the ways I could work with him to learn whether the problem was an unusual, one-time occurrence or whether some more pervading issue required me to address this new set of symptoms.

But the following day, something odd happened. The "one-time occurrence" with Sam happened again, this time with a Korean War veteran named Victor.

Victor was in the middle of a violent firefight in Korea when he saw his best friend, Charlie, drop to the ground some yards from him. After the fight was over, he walked to where his friend had fallen and found Charlie's bloody, lifeless body. For the decades since then, the image of his friend's body came to him regularly and he felt profound sadness. As he told me the story, his whole body shook and he sobbed with his face in his hands. I asked him how sad he felt and he said, "A 10," the severest possible rating on the 10-point scale I use with many of my patients. Victor's sadness was bare and raw because he had no anger or guilt to protect himself from feeling its intensity.

I knew core-focused EMDR would help reduce his deep sadness, so I administered a set of eye movements and told him to keep the bloody image of his friend in his mind. The sadness immediately started to come down and his body stopped shaking. "7 now," he said, his body relaxing. I administered another set of eye movements and he said he was down to "a 2 or 3." After more eye movements, he closed his eyes and kept them closed for a few minutes. A smile crept across his face. I was puzzled by this odd behavior, concerned that my patient may have stopped the process to think about something else—highly unusual in core-focused EMDR.

When he opened his eyes, he looked at me, relaxed in his chair, and said slowly, with his brow wrinkled in disbelief, "I saw him."

"You saw who?" I asked.

"Charlie," he replied. "I guess it was his spirit."

I was stunned, but encouraged him to go on. My thoughts were darting about trying to make sense of what was going on. How could a second veteran be having a similar incredible hallucination within two days?

Victor continued, "He looked very happy, and he had a big smile. He looked healthy, not bloody and dead the way I've always remembered him since Korea. Doc, he said to me 'It's OK.' When he said that, I really felt like it was OK."

As Victor was leaving at the end of the session, I shook his hand and he reached out and hugged me with his other arm. Victor had never expressed any affection before.

After he left my office, I closed the door slowly behind him, lost in thought. During my eight years on the unit, I had never seen one of these imaginative hallucinations that resolved the patient's traumatic losses immediately and decisively; now I had seen two in two days.

A week later it happened again with another vet, then another. Within three weeks, I had witnessed six of these remarkable occurrences, all with the same reported vividness, the certainty the vets expressed that it was real, the positive assurances they reported from the person who had died, and the unprecedented resolution of long-standing, intractable traumatic grief. About 15 percent of my patients were experiencing them. Astonishingly, while I had become accustomed to seeing the patients' sadness and associated feelings reduce when I used core-focused EMDR, after most of these unusual sessions, the patients left the office joyous.

The scientist in me was reassuring me that there was some reasonable explanation for the phenomenon. I leafed through the notes I had written immediately after all of my sessions and located those describing the six sessions in which these odd scenes played out. I compared them carefully, looking for common themes. I then examined other session notes with similar veterans to see whether I could see any differences.

Then I saw it, a clear difference in the procedure I used with the patients who had the experience. I had been following this sequence: I helped them come to a peak in their sadness using core-focused EMDR, then started to bring it down with additional sets of eye movement. In the cases in which the experience occurred, I provided another set of eye movements without any specific instruction. After this last set of eye movements, the experience occurred.

I theorized about what was probably happening. As long as the patient was focused on the anger and guilt, the sadness remained buried. Core-focused EMDR was uncovering the sadness and most patients were fully addressing it for the first time. After they processed the sadness and it started to lose its intensity, the distracting emotions were set aside and an additional EMDR set without instruction seemed to open them to this apparently natural experience. I later began to call this open state of mind the "receptive mode."

I Intentionally Induce the Experience with a Patient

I wondered whether that combination was the key. The only way to find out was to try it intentionally with a patient. The effect had been so healing and happened so quickly that I felt comfortable trying to help other patients experience it. Even though I had no idea what was causing it, it seemed to work.

So the next day when I met with Gary, a patient who had intensive grief from the death of his daughter, Julie, I resolved to try to help him experience the same healing.

Gary had lost his daughter when she was 13 years old. She had been severely oxygen deprived at birth and never developed mentally beyond the abilities of a six-month-old child. Gary loved her dearly and included her in activities whenever he could. He often took her dancing because she loved music.

One evening, Gary and his wife went out for dinner without their daughter. On the drive home, they passed an ambulance going in the opposite direction. When they arrived home, they learned that their daughter was in the ambulance; she had suffered a severe heart attack. They rushed to the hospital where they learned that her heart had stopped beating for some time and she had been placed on life support to help her breathe. After a few weeks, she showed some signs of breathing on her own, so Gary and his wife made the hopeful decision to take her off the respirator. The day she was taken off the respirator, she struggled briefly to breathe, then died in Gary's arms.

Gary sat in my office crying softly as he finished telling me his story. I explained the new procedure to him and the results other patients had achieved. He was interested in giving it a try, but was sure it wouldn't work for him because he was an atheist and didn't believe in such things.

I used core-focused EMDR to allow him to get in touch with his deep sadness. When the sadness reached its peak, I used eye movements to begin to reduce it. As the sadness started to come down, I asked him to think of his daughter in a general way and to go with whatever happened. I administered a set of eye movements and he closed his eyes. He sat quietly for a few minutes. Then he opened his eyes with a look of amazement.

"I saw my daughter. She was playing happily in a beautiful garden alive with rich and radiant bright colors. She looked healthy and seemed to move around without the physical problems she had when alive." He continued with surprise and delight on his face. "She looked at me and I could feel her love for me."

We talked more about his experience. Gary was convinced that his daughter was still alive, although in a very different place. But he still felt sad because he missed her. I told him to keep that thought in mind while I did another set of eye movements. After the eye movements, Gary closed his eyes and in a few moments opened them with a smile. "I was in the garden again and I could see Julie looking at me. She said to me, 'I'm still with you, Daddy.'" He paused and looked at me. "That was really wonderful. You know, she couldn't talk when she was alive."

Gary left the session feeling joyous and reconnected to his daughter.

After he had gone, I wrote my session notes, feeling elated. Whatever was happening, the experience was healing grief, quickly and dramatically.

During the next several months, I was able to induce the experience with 98 percent reliability by following the sequence precisely, and I was shocked anew every time it happened. Actually, I was more shocked every time. Whatever was happening, from whatever source, the procedure was resolving my patients' grief and traumatic losses. They most often left the sessions in a joyous state.

The Experience Has Striking Similarities to NDEs and ADCs

After one of my sessions, I remembered a book I had read years earlier and dismissed as nonsense at the time. It was *Life after Life,* by Raymond Moody. Dr. Moody wrote that people who are clinically dead, then revive, often report unusual experiences. Some believe they moved through a tunnel, saw a bright light, experienced beautiful landscapes, or saw and communicated with deceased relatives. Dr. Moody used the term near-death experiences, or NDEs, for these phenomena. He reported that they happen spontaneously when a person is closest to death and that they are often life changing.

I also had later read *Reunions: Visionary Encounters with Departed Loved Ones* in which he described his subjects' experiences with deceased loved ones and friends. Dr. Moody induced the experience by using the method of "mirror gazing," which was developed by the ancient Greeks. In his original study, he reported a 50 percent success rate. At the time, I completely dismissed his descriptions, convinced that his work had no credibility. I did not consider the phenomenon again until very recently.

Intrigued by my recollection of Dr. Moody's descriptions of NDEs, I located the old copy of *Life after Life* in my library. I leafed through it and was amazed to see that many of the elements of the NDE were identical to the experiences my patients were reporting in my office. I had read articles by scientists who argued that these NDEs are hallucinations resulting from the neurology of a dying brain, but all of my patients experiencing the same types of phenomena had brains that were as alive during the experience as they had been before they closed their eyes. Something was happening other than a dying brain; it had to be part of the living, healthy, conscious brain.

That impression has been strengthened by experience. In the years since rereading Dr. Moody's book, I have talked to many hundreds of patients who have experienced NDEs, and the opinion I held years ago that the accounts are nonsense has been successfully challenged again and again by the compelling testimonies these normal, everyday people give about their remarkable life-changing experiences.

As I continued my search of the literature, I chanced upon Bill and Judy Guggenheim's *Hello from Heaven!*, which describes after-death communications (ADCs). These experiences are not at all rare, occurring in 20 percent of the population, the authors stated. Their descriptions of ADCs were identical to my patients' descriptions of their experiences, except that the ADCs the Guggenheims described always occurred randomly and spontaneously. In fact, they even made the argument that these experiences cannot be purposefully induced. I used that similarity to begin calling what my patients were experiencing "induced after-death communications," or IADCs.

My patients' experiences, along with the experiences reported by the Guggenheims, forced me to rethink my opinion of Dr. Moody's *Reunions*. Perhaps he was talking about a real phenomenon that was beyond my ability to accept as possible.

The Effects Hold Up over Time

Three months had gone by since I had induced the first IADC with Sam. I wondered whether the remarkable transformation I had seen in him had diminished. I expected his decrease in sadness to hold over time, but strongly suspected that his feeling of a joyous reconnection to Le would fade as most hallucinations do. In a follow-up with Sam, I asked him how he was feeling about his experience after three months. I was surprised when he told me that the feelings of reconnection with Le had not changed. In fact, he had been able, for the first time, without any assistance, to relate to his own daughter in a much more open and loving way because of the experience.

That was more than eight years ago. I recently talked with Sam, and he explained that he continues to feel a profound reconnection to Le. His relationship with his daughter has improved greatly. "I'm making up for lost time with her," he said buoyantly. He added that he had believed in an afterlife before the experience, but since then, "It has proved to me beyond a shadow of doubt that the afterlife is a definite reality."

I also followed up with Gary, the patient with whom I did the first intentional induction. He reported to me a year after the session that he continued to feel reconnected to his daughter. He was also convinced that "People don't really die; they just take on a different form and live in a different place, which is very beautiful."

The experience was changing patients' lives in a single session, and the effect was holding up over time. I began to wonder whether any of my interns or the other psychologists might be able to help their patients have the same experiences.

3

Teaching Other Psychotherapists to Induce After-Death Communications

> I have never let schooling interfere with my education.
>
> —Mark Twain

After several more weeks of watching one patient after another resolve their traumatic losses and grief through IADCs, I decided it was time to tell at least one of the other psychologists on the post-traumatic stress disorder unit about what was happening. I needed to know whether anyone else had seen something similar, whether another experienced psychologist might have an explanation for it, and, most important, whether someone would be willing to use the procedure and replicate the results.

I thought about it for several days before finding the courage to describe it to someone in the unit. After all, telling another behavioral scientist that my patients were talking to the dead was a little scary. But the fact was that whatever was going on was healing grief with such predictability and power that I had to share it with the other professionals on the unit. We had been having regular long discussions for years about how we could more effectively help these veterans alleviate the unimaginable pain they were suffering from combat-related post-traumatic stress disorder. This was working.

One morning I walked into the office of Karaina, the therapist for whom I had the most respect and confidence. I closed the door and quietly sat down. She asked immediately, "What's wrong?"

"I need to share something with you. I want your honest professional opinion."

"Sure."

"OK, here it is. Many of my vets are saying they're having experiences during EMDR sessions that are reducing their symptoms dramatically in one session."

"Right," she said. "That's from core-focused EMDR. I've been using it since you showed it to us and at least two others are too. We're all getting the same incredibly rapid results you are."

"Well, I'm getting more than that now. They're telling me they're communicating with the dead." I looked at her to see her reaction.

"Wonderful. So that's what's reducing the symptoms so dramatically, right?"

"Yes, in a way I've never seen before. Now I'm not suggesting they really are communicating with the dead."

"Oh, I know what you're talking about," she said smiling. "That's like an ADC. Have you ever heard of that?"

"Well, actually I have. I found a book titled *Hello from Heaven!*—"

She interrupted. "I have a copy. I had an ADC myself when I was a teenager."

I was relieved and energized. I asked her to tell me the story. As she told it, I sat in rapt attention.

"I was 14 when my 20-year-old sister died from a rare type of cancer that had spread throughout her body. It disfigured her very badly in the last months. She left behind two small children. Her death about did me in. My parents had divorced just before this and I was depressed about that already, so when my sister was told she was going to die, I didn't know if I was going to make it.

"After she died, I went through the worst period of my life. I honestly felt like ending my life was the only way to stop the horrible feelings I had all day. Then, one night while I was asleep, I saw my sister in a dream. She looked happy and radiant and was healthy again, and she was surrounded by little children. She said to me, 'You want to come with me, don't you?' I said, 'Yes.' My sister said, 'It's not your time. You need to stay there and take care of my kids and Mom. I'll come back for you when it's time.'

"When I woke up that morning, I could remember the dream like it was a real conversation. I felt completely different after that. The depression was gone. I followed her advice and went on with my life, but from that day on, I felt like I had a sense of purpose and responsibility. I raised her children as my own and cared for Mom after she developed some serious medical problems. And here I am today."

Karaina encouraged me to continue exploring this new therapy method and volunteered to try using it herself. I was elated. From that day on, Karaina became my confidant and comrade as the discovery continued to unfold.

Karaina's Patient Has an IADC in Her Office

The next day, we met and I explained the IADC procedure. She understood how different it is from standard EMDR and the importance of developing a receptive, open mind in the patient after the core-focused EMDR. She was an experienced, very capable EMDR therapist, so, after an hour or so, she felt ready to give it a try.

Two days later, Karaina strolled into my office, grinning. "It worked. It was just like you described."

She sat on the edge of a chair and leaned toward me. "I had a session with one of my long-term Vietnam vets. A new soldier had just joined his unit and everyone, including my vet, was teasing him because he was green. A couple of days later, the new soldier was killed in his first firefight, shot in the head. My vet saw his body with a gaping mortal wound to his head. He's been suffering extreme guilt for teasing the new soldier and from the intrusive images of the wound.

"During the core-focused EMDR, as usual I ignored the guilt and went for the sadness. His sadness kept increasing until it peaked and started back down. I did an extra set of eye movements to increase his receptivity and relaxation, just as you suggested, and it happened.

"He said he saw the dead soldier's smiling face and somehow got a message, but he wasn't sure how, that the guy knew my vet's teasing was out of affection. The dead guy communicated that he was all right and that my vet shouldn't feel bad. My vet was really befuddled. He had no idea what it was, but here's the great part. He said to me, 'You know, it's strange. I don't feel sad any more, not a drop. And I don't feel guilty. And when I try to remember the old image of the wound, I can't even get it to come into my head. I just remember his smiling face telling me he's OK.'"

We were beside ourselves. We talked as long as we could before our next appointments, knowing we were at the beginning of something more wonderful for our patients than we could have imagined.

When Karaina left, I stood looking out the window. She had replicated my results. Whatever this was, it was a capacity hidden in ordinary, every-day people that we could help patients find deep inside themselves. Once they tapped into it, this remarkable capability would emerge naturally and heal the patients' grief. And someone else had seen it work the same way I had.

But something kept surfacing in my thoughts. In our talk about what happened, Karaina seemed to be willing to entertain the possibility that these IADC sessions could really be communications with the deceased. Her own experience as a teenager had profoundly affected her thinking in the same way the IADCs were affecting my patients. They were all cer-tain their experiences were real after-death communications.

An Intern Learns to Induce IADCs

A few weeks later, I decided to introduce IADC therapy to one of my most competent predoctoral interns. "Intern" suggests a young, naïve novice still wet behind the ears. Lucy was not. She was one of the most com-petent interns I have ever worked with. This is the story of what happened.

Lucy had already experienced success with EMDR and was eager to learn how to use it in IADC therapy. I explained to her that I use EMDR differently to induce an IADC. She was quick to grasp the differences. After a couple of hours of introduction to core-focused EMDR and IADC therapy, she was willing to try it with one of her patients.

The patient she chose was suffering from intrusive images and guilt over an incident that happened during his tour in Vietnam. He was riding in the passenger seat of a truck when he saw a 13-year-old Vietnamese boy run out in front of the truck. He yelled to the driver, "Watch out! Stop!" But the driver didn't see the boy and the truck hit him.

They got out of the truck and found the boy dead. The guilt he felt over not being able to stop the accident and the intrusive images of the boy's body gave him nightmares and uncontrollable waking images for 28 years.

I coached Lucy prior to her session with this veteran. She went to her office for the appointment and I waited with great anticipation. Only one other therapist had successfully induced an IADC at that point. Could it be that we were the only two in the world who would see it?

At the end of the session, she came into my office obviously disappointed. She said, "It didn't work. My patient felt some sadness, but kept wanting to talk about his guilt, so we spent most of the session discussing it."

I explained to Lucy that the patient was avoiding his sadness and that she should have said, "It's important to stay with your sadness." I had learned that in using core-focused EMDR and the extension into IADC therapy, the therapist must keep the patient on track, at times aggressively.

Lucy understood. The next day when she met with the patient again, she kept him on target with core-focused EMDR. The patient's sadness at first escalated, then began to come down. She asked the patient, "What would you like to say to that boy?"

The patient answered, shaking his head slowly, "I'm sorry. I'm sorry."

Lucy did a set of eye movements to induce receptivity. He closed his eyes. After a few minutes, he opened them with a wide grin.

"I saw him as clear as day. He had the biggest smile you could imagine and seemed to have a glow all around him. He was happier than anyone I have ever seen before. He didn't speak, but I knew for sure what he was saying. He was saying that I was a good person and it wasn't my fault."

By this time, the patient was relaxed, happy, and talkative. She had never seen him like that.

After the patient left, Lucy came into my office excitedly and described what had happened. "I still can't believe it. I couldn't know all of it would work until I was able to do it myself."

After Lucy's experience, I confidently taught the therapy method to 30 other interns over an eight-year period. They all had the same results. The interns learned the procedure easily, were ecstatic to see it work, and were making differences in patients' lives.

Soon after Lucy's experience, I arranged with Karaina to have her do the IADC procedure with me as the subject. I had two successful IADCs. Listening to patient reports about the IADCs from the outside was remarkable; experiencing them twice myself, however, was breathtaking. Like my patients, I was surprised by the content of the experiences. In both instances, it was completely different from what I had expected, even though, by that time, I had heard my patients describe many of their IADCs. The experiences left me more enthusiastic than ever about the wonderful gift we had been given.

The next months were filled with exploration and wonder. Other colleagues learned to use the procedure and had the same results. And as patients having the IADC experiences came to number in the hundreds, we began to understand more about this remarkable capacity hidden in normal, everyday people.

4

New Ideas in the Treatment of Grief

All of the art of living lies in the fine mingling of letting go and holding on.

—Henry Havelock Ellis

As we successfully induced more IADCs, I came to realize that it is the experience of reconnection that heals. The painful sadness is based on an underlying sense of disconnection from the deceased. People experiencing grief say things like "I feel that a part of me has been taken away" or "I feel incomplete now."

The sense of disconnection, then, results in the core sadness. The other emotions (anger, numbness, and guilt) defend the person against feeling the painful sadness. The experience of reconnection in the IADC seems to resolve the sense of disconnection, thereby diminishing or eradicating the sadness. The accompanying defense emotions simply vanish; they are no longer necessary.

This experience of reconnection is illustrated in the words most commonly heard after an IADC: "I feel reconnected to her" and "I feel whole again." The experience of reconnection is central in resolving grief through IADC therapy.

I recently became aware that this renewed bond brought about by IADC therapy complements a growing trend in grief therapy. For the greater part of a century, standard grief therapy has insisted that the bereaved must extinguish emotional ties to deceased loved ones and replace the attachment to the deceased with other people and interests. Grief therapists now realize, however, that people simply do not separate psychologically from their deceased loved ones. Instead, they continue to think about, feel for, speak to, and even ask for advice from them. The new approach to grief therapy now emerging acknowledges this reality and helps patients develop this natural aspect of grieving into a healthy continuing bond with the deceased.

The Change in Grief Therapy Now Taking Place

A colleague once told me he was taught in medical school that grief usually lasts from three to six months. That is a very misleading guideline because grief is a highly individual matter influenced by factors unique to every grieving person, such as the ages of the deceased and survivor, the survivor's support system, the survivor's relationship to the deceased, and the cause or circumstances of the death. More important, grief usually never fully resolves.

Most grief counselors agree that it takes people from one to two years to feel sufficiently reconciled to a loss that they can again find enjoyment in living without their loved one. It takes even longer when the grief is for a deceased child or a spouse of many years, and reminders of the loss can continue to trigger the grief emotions for a lifetime.

The primary emotional components of grief beyond the initial stages of shock and numbing are generally feelings of sadness, guilt, and anger. The bond between the living is love, but when a loved one dies, the bond is pain. Helping a client work through the pain is complicated by guilt and fears of complete disconnection with the deceased. Guilt can be associated with a wide variety of issues, but most commonly it results from a sense of having unfinished business with the deceased, such as never having expressed love or said "I love you," having unresolved conflicts, and even having been responsible or feeling responsible for the death. Generally, those who grieve also feel intense anger because someone very important has been taken away. Both guilt and anger can be related to attributions of blame and responsibility.

Freud wrote that the goal of grief therapy is to assist survivors in severing the bonds with the deceased and disengaging emotionally so they can construct a new life devoid of all ties to the deceased. Therapy sessions involve a long series of confrontations to help the survivor realize the finality of the loss and let go of any attachment to the deceased. In this conception of grief therapy, those unable to sever all ties fail and thus remain miserable and dysfunctional.

Standard grief therapy since Freud has held to that conception of grief work. It normally takes survivors through this sequence:

1. Help survivors accept the reality that the loved ones are dead by having them talk about the circumstances of the death and issues associated with the loss. This assists survivors to get through the initial shock and numbing phase of grief.

2. Help them withdraw emotionally from the deceased by supporting them in expressing and working through the usual feelings associated with the loss: anger, guilt, and sadness.

3. Help them adjust to a life without the deceased by learning to live their lives in different ways and develop new relationships.

4. Provide support during more difficult times such as birthdays, anniversaries, and holidays.

The goal of standard grief therapy in this conception is to help survivors accept their loss and get on with their lives. The process often requires years of counseling with limited success. Recently, however, a growing number of grief therapists have begun to suggest that patients who *maintain their bonds* with the deceased often adjust better to their loss. These observations are resulting in a reconsideration of grief and grief therapy.

In 1996, Dennis Klass, Phyllis Silverman, and Steven Nickman published *Continuing Bonds: New Understandings of Grief,* which challenged mainstream thinking about grief. The book's 22 well-respected scholars in the field of grief and loss offer a radical new model for understanding and treating grief. Their model presages the grief therapy exemplified in IADC therapy.

The authors explain that current ideas about grief are based more on cultural norms than scientific data. In the twentieth century, Western societies' emphasis on individual autonomy over social interdependence did much to shape our ideas about grief. The goal of mainstream grief treatments has been to help survivors maximize their autonomy by fully accepting the finality of death and severing their bonds with the deceased. The assumption has been that the survivor will only then be able to establish new relationships and a life without the deceased. Pathological grief has been assumed to result from not letting go of the deceased emotionally.

The authors of *Continuing Bonds* cite many clinical observations and research outcomes that challenge these assumptions. They report that survivors who maintain a continuing bond with the deceased appear to be better adjusted psychologically throughout the grieving process. Continuing bonds are fluid, changing, and affirming. They assist survivors in dealing with their ongoing issues in life and are integrated into current relationships, providing survivors with context and meaning.

These continuing bonds are distinguished, however, from pathological denial in which the survivor's only connection with the deceased is static, unchanging, and stuck in what once was and can never be again. The best criterion for judging whether the connection is pathological or helpful is the person's quality of life.

Examples of continuing bonds the authors cite:

1. dreaming of the deceased
2. talking to the deceased
3. believing the deceased is watching the survivor
4. keeping items that belonged to the deceased
5. visiting the grave
6. frequently thinking of the deceased

While some of the authors describe a few continuing bonds that appear to be true after-death communications, on the whole, these scholars chose not to speculate on the ultimate nature of these experiences. Instead, they prefer to collectively label these experiences, "inner representations of the deceased." (The articles in *Continuing Bonds* were submitted before the publication of the Guggenheims' survey of spontaneous ADCs in *Hello from Heaven!*)

IADCs Have Changed Our Approach to Grief Therapy

IADC therapy is congruent with the focus on continuing bonds, providing a richer, more personal, experiential sense of the continuing bond. The IADC experience allows patients suffering from grief and traumatic loss to resolve the issues rapidly through an experiential reconnection with those who have died.

Instead of encouraging acceptance of the feelings of disconnection and withdrawal from emotional attachment to the deceased, IADC therapy actually provides psychological resolution through the profound, life-changing experience of *reconnection* with the deceased. Their sense of love and unbroken connection is renewed by an uplifting experience that gives them the feeling of a different but satisfying and permanent new relationship with the deceased. They rebuild meaning through the new relationship, and they continue their bond knowing their loved one is OK and imminent.

The experience of reconnection heals.

Sally's Case: "He said he would come for me when it was my time."

"I just cry for no reason." Sally wept, clutching a wet handkerchief. Her depression wasn't responding to medications, so she was referred to me. As we talked, it became clear she was deeply in grief over her father's death five years before. She had stayed by his side for months while the cancerous growth on the side of his neck grew, sapping his life away day after painful day. She wept bitterly. The images of her father dying with the cancerous growth on his neck wouldn't leave her.

When she was ready, I used EMDR to reduce her overwhelming sadness and the pain of the images of her father dying.

After the sadness had decreased, I initiated the IADC procedure and asked her to close her eyes and go with whatever happened. The first induction did not result in an IADC. On the second induction, however, after a moment with her eyes still closed, she said, "I can see him. He looks healthy again. He looks happy." She smiled and paused. "Grandma and grandpa are with him. . . . and two of my aunts and my uncle who died long ago."

She paused, gazing inward. "They're partying, laughing. . . . Oh, they're enjoying themselves. They're in a room filled with bright white light."

She opened her eyes and looked at me. "I could somehow feel their happiness." She said excitedly, "I was wishing I could be with my father . . . I don't mean suicide. I just wanted to be with him now, but I know I can't."

I started another IADC procedure while she held that thought in mind. The same scene came back, but there was more. "He walked right up to me and said he was still with me in a very important way, that I should continue to take care of my children, and that he would come for me when it was my time." She smiled warmly through her tears.

When Sally left my office that day, all of her grief and pain over the death of her father were gone. As she was leaving, she said, "That was absolutely amazing. As soon as I felt I was reconnected with them, my sadness vanished. I know that was really them. I'll have to tell my brother about this. I know he'll think I'm a raving lunatic, but I don't care; I feel great."

From that day on, Sally no longer experienced any symptoms of depression.

Some have questioned my observation that grief completely resolves in this way after an IADC. They point out that if someone's child dies, even a loving IADC reconnection will not keep the parent from feeling a profound sense of sadness at times, such as the day she would have graduated from high school or his birthday. I agree that an IADC experience does not substitute for those shared experiences that can never come to be. Those losses are, however, secondary to the primary loss: "My child is gone. She's completely disconnected from me."

After IADCs, people who have suffered tragic losses no longer feel disconnected, so although they still experience the more secondary feelings of loss on occasions such as birthdays and the anniversary of the death, the sadness at those times is much more readily tolerated because the bereaved doesn't feel the deep and more painful sadness associated with a sense of complete disconnection. The survivor is able to deal with the grief at those times in a more adaptive way, and is often able to honor and fondly remember the lost loved one.

How IADCs Heal Traumatic Grief

In post-traumatic stress disorder, the patient relives the trauma over and over. Flashes of scenes appear at any time and can begin to replay the entire trauma. Many try to stop the reliving through distractions or anesthetizing consciousness with drugs or alcohol. We discovered that EMDR helps post-traumatic stress disorder patients reduce the intensity of intrusive memories from traumatic events by taking the reliving component out of the memory. Patients often remark that they can still remember the trauma, but it feels like it happened a long time ago or as though it had been in a story.

IADCs help our patients heal traumatic images by providing a positive image that naturally replaces the negative one. Very often, the deceased's wounds, disfigurement, or distressed face are replaced by images of peace, calm, and a happy, smiling face. Patients often remark that they can't even remember the traumatic image as it was. When they try to remember it, they see the positive image instead. I believe that this may be why IADC results hold up so well over time.

Gene's Case: "All I can see is her smiling at me and speaking to me."

Gene was 19 years old when his mother suffered a massive heart attack while they sat on the couch together. She said she didn't feel well, clutched her chest, and fell sideways onto him. Panic-stricken, he realized she wasn't breathing and gave her mouth-to-mouth resuscitation, but she was gone. Her eyes were open, with the pupils rolled back, and her face had lost muscle tone. He called the awful image that stayed with him her "death face."

For decades, all he could remember about his mother was the death face. He avoided thinking about her because when he thought of her, he would see only the death face. As a result, he was unable to process his grief.

Gene sat in my office describing the death face, shaking his head vigorously as if that would shake the memory out of his mind. He had no tears, though. He protested that he was over it, but wished he could get rid of the death face.

He agreed to let me use core-focused EMDR to try to reduce the sadness and accompanying image. I administered some eye movements and his sadness increased, along with the clarity of the death-face image. He was getting in touch with the intense feelings he had buried since her death. When the sadness peaked, he was wracked with sobs.

"Stay with that feeling. Don't let go now," I said, and administered another set of eye movements. The sadness started to come back down. After another set of eye movements, he closed his eyes, and the IADC began.

"I can see my mother," he said with his eyes closed. "She's dressed in white with tremendous light all around her. She looks young, maybe in her twenties, and she's wearing an outdated dress."

After a few more seconds, he opened his eyes. "She said she's very proud of me, that I should continue to be a good person, and she would see me again when it was my time. Dr. Botkin, I feel warm all over, like I haven't felt for years."

I asked him if he could recall the death face. He thought for a moment. "I can't see it. I'm trying to see it and I can't see it. All I can see is her smiling at me and speaking to me like she did just now when I saw her. It's a wonderful feeling."

From that time on, Gene insisted he couldn't remember the death face. His only memories of his mother were warm and positive.

Frieda's Case: "It made me feel like he's all right . . . life's all right."

Frieda's story is another illustration of the healing effect of the simple, powerful message "I'm OK," and of a pleasant image replacing a gruesome one.

Frieda was a student nurse who came to me because she was having intrusive images of a death that were interfering with her life. During her nurse training, she was on rotation in the emergency room one afternoon when a five-year-old boy was brought in on the verge of death. He had been hit by a car, then run over by another car. His body and the gurney on which he lay as they rushed him through the emergency ward were soaked with blood and he was unconscious. She and the emergency room team worked feverishly to try to save his life, but it was in vain. His injuries were too severe and he died.

Frieda was in shock. She hurried home, locked herself in her room, and cried for hours. That night, she couldn't sleep. The intrusive images of the boy's mangled body and the blood kept coming back to her. For the next several nights, she slept fitfully but the images came to her and she would awaken in tears. She decided she was not cut out to be a nurse and prepared to leave the school.

She came to me because she knew I specialized in helping patients with traumatic memories. After she told me the story, we started the IADC procedure. I first used EMDR on the images until they started to fade. Then I used core-focused EMDR to open the sadness that was at the core of her trauma. The sadness increased with successive eye movements, then started to come back down. I instructed her to be open to anything that came to her as she thought about the child. I administered another set of eye movements, after which she closed her eyes.

With her eyes closed, she described what she was seeing. "I can see the little boy. He's healthy and playing in a beautiful field with other children." She sat quietly for a moment, then opened her eyes.

"What happened?" I asked.

"He looked directly at me and smiled. It was a wonderful smile, and I had the feeling he knew what I was going through. It made me feel . . . It made me feel like he's all right . . . life's all right."

"When you think of him, what do you see now?"

"I just see that wonderful, warm smile. I can remember his bloody body, but it's like an old memory of something that happened a long time ago and is over now, and I don't have the feeling I am going to cry."

She paused and looked at me in wonder. "In fact, I don't feel sad at all about it."

When she came back for a session a week later, she told me that all negative images of the boy had vanished, but she kept seeing his wonderful smile when she thought about him. She had recommitted herself to nursing and had decided to become an emergency room nurse because she had something important to offer people—her strength.

IADCs Take Continuing Bonds to a Higher Level

The IADC experience allows grieving patients to develop their sense of a continuing bond with the deceased. The result of this new orientation is a marked reduction in sadness and accompanying negative emotions, and often a new feeling of contentment. IADCs, in other words, take the new orientation toward grief therapy that fosters patients' natural, healthy tendency to develop continuing bonds with the deceased to a higher, experiential level.

The next chapter explains the most common types of IADCs we've repeatedly seen and the remarkable power they have to help patients develop continuing, healthy bonds with the deceased, often in one session.

5

Common Observations in IADCs

Knowledge speaks, but wisdom listens.

—Jimi Hendrix

The number of successful IADCs induced by my colleagues, interns, and me continued to increase as we jubilantly watched many patients walk out of our offices happy and healed. After they numbered in the thousands, we came to understand the characteristics of these wonderful experiences that foster development of healthy, continuing bonds with the deceased.

We had learned that the IADC always unfolds naturally, usually in ways neither the patient nor the psychotherapist could ever have predicted, wished for, or imagined. The patient and the psychotherapist are not in control of the content of the experience. Remarkably, in spite of that, the results are nearly always inspiring, loving, and full of forgiveness or insights that bring about healing in virtually all of the patients who experience them.

In this chapter are examples of the common content other therapists and I have heard in reports by patients who have experienced IADCs.

They Normally Last Only a Few Seconds, but Duration Is Not as Important as Content

The IADC experience itself normally lasts only five to 20 seconds, but may extend to ten or 15 minutes or longer. The duration is not important to the profound healing; the content is. Some patients experience the IADC immediately upon closing their eyes. Others sit quietly for a few seconds before experiencing it.

Interestingly, some patients seem to lose their sense of time as they experience the IADC. In one case, the patient closed his eyes after the set of eye movements and opened them in less than five seconds. I thought, "OK, nothing happened. Let's see what the problem might have been." The patient then described a lengthy, elaborate IADC that seemed as though it would have taken several minutes to unfold.

Out of curiosity, I asked him how long he thought he had been sitting with his eyes closed. He said, "Oh, maybe two or three minutes."

In other cases, patients have sat with their eyes closed for minutes and, when I asked what happened, reported, "I saw him smiling," or some other experience that would have taken only a few seconds to unfold. These patients consistently underestimated the amount of time they had their eyes closed.

Experiencers Insist the Experiences Are Not Imagination

Nearly all of those who experience IADCs assert that these experiences are markedly different from dreams, imagination, or fantasy. Most insist that they actually saw, heard, touched, or smelled things with their senses, but that the sensations were not physical. In other words, they knew they were inner or mental, but felt them to be as real as anything physical.

The best way to explain that difference is to allow one of the patients who experienced an IADC to explain it. Her name is Margie. I include her descriptions here because she was exceptionally articulate and insightful about her experience, and I found that our discussion helped me understand how patients experience IADCs.

Margie explained that while normal, waking consciousness is preoccupied with sensory input from the physical environment, her IADC was based on sensory input that was purely mental. She emphatically claimed, however, that even though her IADC was a mental event, it was no less real than any physical event.

Her IADC was also qualitatively different from all of her other mental events such as dreams, images created while in a hypnotic trance, imagination and fantasies, hallucinations from a fever she had as a child, and even an LSD trip she had experienced many years before. For her, these other experiences were not real, but her IADC was.

She went on to describe the communication in her IADC. Communication did occur, but not in the usual physical sense, where sounds or sound waves are emitted and received, she said. Instead, words were conveyed mentally, but in a clearer manner than physical communication. She also said that emotions were clearly transmitted along with the words. She stumbled somewhat in her attempt to put her experience into words because it occurred on a level that she said "goes beyond words."

I then asked her how she could be so sure that her IADC was a real experience and not some fantastic mental creation on her part. She responded by saying she knew it was real because she couldn't make it go the way she wanted it to, and when she tried to control the experience, it didn't work. As the IADC unfolded, it was completely different from what she had expected. She was convinced that the experience was not of her own making.

The following case of Rebecca is an example of the IADC experiencer's surprise at how real the experience seems.

Rebecca's Case: "I don't know if that was all in my imagination. It was so real."

Rebecca, a highly educated professional, sat in my office solemnly telling me the story about her daughter, Lorna, who had died about six months before Rebecca came to me. Rebecca hoped to have some relief from the tremendous grief she was feeling over her daughter's death. I went through the usual explanation of EMDR and told her that she must be willing to allow herself to feel her deepest sadness without drawing back from it. I said that I would keep her focused on it during the therapy session, even when the sadness became difficult for her. I then explained that some people experience ADCs and gave her a brief description. She agreed to participate.

I began the IADC procedure by telling her to pay attention to her sadness about her daughter as I administered a set of eye movements. When I stopped the movements, I told her to close her eyes.

After a moment, I asked, "How are you feeling?"

"Sad," she said, as a tear trickled from her eye.

"Open your eyes and I'll do another set of eye movements. Stay with the sadness."

I performed the eye movement procedure and asked her to close her eyes. She began to weep.

"You're doing what you need to do," I said. "We'll do another set of eye movements. Stay with the feeling."

She opened her eyes and I administered another set of eye movements. This core-focused EMDR continued through three more sets until she was sobbing with grief. I knew that she was fully accessing the core sadness. After two more eye movement sets to reduce the sadness, her sobbing began to diminish, showing that she was ready for the IADC induction.

"How are you feeling now?"

"Better, but I loved her so much," she said, looking at me intently.

"Let's do another set of eye movements. Just relax and let whatever comes to your mind come freely." I provided eye movements to relax her and help her enter a receptive state.

She closed her eyes and sat quietly. After a few seconds, she opened her eyes and reported to me what had happened. "I could feel Lorna being with me, not strongly, but I don't know whether I was just remembering her."

"You're doing fine," I said. "Stay with that and we'll do another set of eye movements."

I did more EMDR eye movements and she closed her eyes.

After a few seconds, with her eyes still closed, she said, "I feel some pressure on my neck and shoulders. My God, it feels like a hug. . . . like Lorna's hugging me." She opened her eyes. "I don't know what to make of this," she said shaking her head. "I can't figure this out. I could feel a hug." She had a broad smile on her tear-stained face and her eyes glistened.

"Stay with that," I said, "and we'll do another set of eye movements."

I completed the eye movement procedure and she closed her eyes.

"Oh, Dr. Botkin," she said, "I heard her saying 'I love you, Mom.' It was her voice." She opened her eyes and looked at me intently. "But I don't know if that was all in my imagination. It was so real."

As we talked about the IADC experience, she said, "I feel calm and at peace for the first time in six months and I don't feel like I'm falling to pieces the way I did. But I'm not sure what to think about what happened."

That is a not an uncommon reaction after the first IADC. Some patients remark that they aren't sure what to believe and describe their experience as being unlike anything they've ever had before in their lives, but they don't quite know how to evaluate it.

When Rebecca met with me a week later, she reported that she was much better about her daughter's death. She was able to talk about her without breaking down, and she didn't awaken in the night sobbing. I suggested we do another IADC induction to address the residual sadness. She agreed.

After a patient has had an IADC induction, the second and subsequent experiences are easily and quickly induced. Her IADC began after a single set of eye movements. She sat quietly with her eyes closed for a few seconds, then opened them and told me what had happened.

"This time I felt her hug again, and when I felt her arms around me I knew this wasn't coming from my own mind. It was her. I was wanting and expecting something totally different, but I know now that this was exactly what I needed." As she was leaving at the end of the session, she said, "Dr. Botkin, the experience said it all, and it answered my questions in a way I couldn't have anticipated."

The Patient and Therapist Are Not in Control of the Experience

The patient is decidedly not in control of what happens during the experience. The therapist is even further removed from the content of the IADC, waiting quietly as the patient experiences the event with closed eyes. The therapist does not speak or lead the patient. The IADC then unfolds unpredictably with no control by the patient; the therapist learns about it from the patient after it has finished.

As a result, the message the person receives is often a surprise and, at times, not what the patient wanted to hear. It is always wise and insightful, however.

That is what happened with Peter, who had a special psychological condition that would have moved his IADC in a very different direction if he had been in control of it.

Peter's Case: "You still don't understand death, but in time you will."

Peter was narcissistic; he needed everything to center on him. At the time he came to me, Peter wanted help coping with his wife's death, which had occurred just two days before our session. He explained to me what had happened.

He and his wife had just finished dinner when she stood uneasily and said to him, "I don't feel well. I'm going out for some air." She walked outside and stood before the long flight of steps that led from the porch to the street, hoping to feel better. A moment later, Peter heard the sound of his wife falling down the stairs.

Peter ran outside and, to his horror, saw her lying motionless at the bottom of the stairs. He ran down to her, breathless, and realized she was unconscious, with a large gash on her head. He ran to the phone and called 911, then hurried back to her to wait.

When the paramedics arrived, he felt they were getting out of the ambulance too slowly. "My God, my wife is dying. Can't you hurry! Do something, quick," he shouted.

When they arrived at the hospital, she was pronounced dead on arrival. He was filled with rage at the paramedics, believing they could have saved her. After he told me the story, he sat in my office enraged, crying, and on the verge of collapse.

I used EMDR to help him calm himself. As I expected, the rage gradually changed to deep sadness. The sadness mounted until he was sobbing and shaking his head; it then started to subside. I used two more sets of eye movements and the IADC experience began while his eyes were closed.

"I can see my wife," he said. "She's beautiful. She's radiant, surrounded by bright light." After a moment, he opened his eyes. "She told me not to be angry with the paramedics. She said she was dead by the time she hit the bottom of the stairs." His tone became agitated. "Then she started telling me what to do with the kids. Do this, do that. I wanted her to talk about me and my feelings, not the kids." Peter's narcissism required that people focus on his needs, not anyone else's.

I said, "OK, let's go back into it and you can tell her how you're feeling. Let's do another set of eye movements and think about her."

We did another set of eye movements; he closed his eyes and sat quietly for a minute. When he opened his eyes, he explained, "She said, 'It's OK. You'll get over it with time. It's OK.' She also said for me to stay away from the new business venture I'm about to begin. And something else. Her father was there. He died years ago. Why was he there?"

"Why don't you ask him?"

We did another set of eye movements and Peter closed his eyes. After a few seconds, he opened them, and explained, "He said, 'I'm here because we are together now. That's the relationship we always had. I'm here because I love my daughter. We do what we have always done.'"

Peter was still sad about his wife's death and wondered why. We agreed he would go back to the scene and ask his father-in-law why he was still feeling sad. I had him do a set of eye movements while Peter thought about his father-in-law. Peter went back into the IADC and asked his father-in-law, "Why do I still feel sad about this?" He reported that his father-in-law replied, "Because you still don't understand death, but in time you will."

Peter reported that his wife was there and that she said, "I love you and will always be with you and the kids."

Peter's IADC is an example of the fact that the patient's desires and psychological condition have no effect on the content of the IADC. If it had been imagination or wishful thinking, he would have, because of his narcissism, created a scene in which he was the center of attention. In fact, he experienced his wife being concerned about their children, not him, and his father-in-law was in the scene when he would have chosen to have his wife focus on him alone.

Peter's IADC also demonstrates that the therapist is able to have the patient return to the IADC. I was able to take Peter back to the experience so he could ask the questions he formulated between IADCs.

The Therapist Can Help the Patient Go Back to Continue the Experience

The patient must be in an open, receptive state, without expectations and without trying to make something happen. The therapist says nothing during the experience and usually hears about what happened only afterward. The therapist can help the patient return to the experience and learn more about it, though, or even help the patient formulate questions to ask during the next IADC experience. The therapist does not lead the patient in any way, however. It is entirely the patient's experience.

After the patient has had the IADC, it is easy to go back to the experience to allow the patient to continue or expand upon what happened. The therapist simply directs another set of eye movements and asks the patient to think about the issue that remains. At that point, it is not necessary to use core-focused EMDR again. Reentry is easy.

Harry's Case: "She said that she was still . . . and always will be . . . with me."

Harry came to me distraught. He felt there was little I could do to help him because much of his problem was harassment from people around him, but he had nowhere else to turn, and suicide was becoming an increasingly attractive alternative.

Tears rolled down Harry's face as he told me his story. Six years before our session, he had been driving with his good friend Martha in a rainstorm when his car slid out of control and slammed into a tree. Martha was killed instantly. Her teenage sons blamed Harry for their mother's death and, in the months after the accident, harassed him and even threatened to kill him. He was guilt-ridden, bereaved, and fearful. Suicide seemed the only alternative to stop the torment.

He agreed to an IADC session and we began. I went through the induction process two times as tears rolled down his face. On the third induction, he closed his eyes, sat quietly for a moment and began to smile, then began to laugh. He kept laughing with his eyes closed for some time as I watched curiously.

After a few minutes, he opened his eyes. "I saw Martha," he began excitedly. "When I first saw her, I said right away I was sorry for what had happened. She said, 'It's OK.' Then she started to joke with me just like we always did. She said, 'Look at me; I'm OK, but I still haven't lost any weight.'" Harry laughed. "Then she told me her children are OK, but I don't know what that means."

"Why don't you ask her?"

He agreed and I took him back into the experience with another IADC to see if he could develop a sense about what she meant. After a few seconds, he opened his eyes and explained, "Martha told me that her children were no longer angry with me and I don't need to worry about them anymore." He paused, filled with emotion. "She also said that she was still . . . and always will be . . . with me."

Harry's feelings of sadness, guilt, and fear all resolved almost immediately. Being able to have Harry reenter the IADC was key to understanding the message and resolving central issues in his grief.

IADCs Provide Insights When the Therapist and Patient Are at an Impasse

There have been times when the patient and I have been at an impasse. The patient was confused and I didn't have enough information to suggest how to get past the obstacle. I learned that all I have to do is induce an IADC with the deceased involved in the grief and have the patient ask for the advice. Every time, without fail, the advice the patient receives is insightful and right on the mark. I began to joke that "The dead make the best therapists."

The Primary Message in IADCs Is "I'm OK"

Those who experience IADCs often remark about how natural and normal the IADC experience is. IADCs aren't populated by cherubim or people in white robes playing harps. The deceased appear to them as they did when alive, although now they are healthy, whole, happy, and often younger. The primary message patients report is also remarkably normal: "I'm OK." That simple statement heals grief.

Hank's story illustrates the grief-healing power of feeling that the deceased is all right.

Hank's Case: "All of our worst fears about death and dying aren't true."

One day in Vietnam, Hank's unit received a report from intelligence that the enemy was transporting weapons in boats on a nearby river. Hank's unit set up on the riverbank that night and, as expected, two boats eventually came down the river. Following orders to fire on any boats coming down the river, they opened fire. When they pulled the boats ashore, they found that they had been occupied by two families out fishing. There were no weapons on board. Everyone on the boats was dead, with many bullet holes through them.

Hank was devastated to see a baby on one of the boats with a bullet hole through its head. The image became the subject of Hank's nightmares for 33 years. Hank had prided himself in not getting caught up in the viciousness of the war, but he realized that it could have been his bullet that killed the baby.

Tears rolled down Hank's face as he finished his story. He was overcome by feelings of sadness and guilt.

I induced an IADC without complication. After a moment, with his eyes closed, Hank described what he saw. "I see a beautiful Vietnamese woman about 30 years old. She's coming to me. It's very odd. I'm sure the baby and this woman are the same person. She's surrounded by radiant white light."

He paused, then continued, "She just said to me, 'You are a kind person.'" He sat quietly for a minute. Then he opened his eyes and reported that she began to leave, but Hank managed to say to her in a way he couldn't explain, "Please don't go." He told me that the woman looked at him and replied, "Don't worry about me; I'm OK," and then said pointedly, "Everything is OK." She then faded away.

All of Hank's issues resolved at that point and he was smiling. He was also profoundly struck by her last statement. "She was telling me that all of our worst fears about death and dying aren't true. I could tell that's what she meant. I didn't just imagine that."

Hank took great comfort in the scene, and the grief that had shrouded him for 33 years and was resistant to psychotherapy resolved from that session on.

Jose's Case: "I feel like a daddy again."

Another patient, Jose, experienced the feeling of reconnection with his only child, an infant daughter, who had been with him for only two months.

Jose was one of my postcombat trauma patients at the VA hospital. He had come to me because he couldn't concentrate; his depression was compounded by alcoholism, nightmares, and recurring images of war. We worked on his traumatic memories and one by one resolved them. Then, one day we began to talk about his infant daughter who had passed away at two months from multiple birth defects. With tears rolling down his cheeks, he agreed to participate in an IADC to help resolve his grief.

I performed the IADC procedure twice. After the second induction, he closed his eyes and in a moment his face changed. He looked a little surprised. "I see her, but she is a healthy, happy teenager. She is surrounded by a bright soft light." He paused for a moment. "She says she is OK and she is fine and happy. She wants me to be happy too." The tears had stopped and he was relaxing in the chair with a grin on his face.

He opened his eyes and said excitedly, "Dr. Botkin, she reached out and gave me a hug with both arms and said, 'I love you.' I feel like a daddy again."

Jose ended the session by saying that before that moment, he never would have believed that could happen. He was sure he had communicated with his daughter. He hugged me and walked out, thanking me over and over. Later, he told me that night he had his best night's sleep in 30 years.

Many IADCs Contain Conversations with the Deceased

Many of the IADCs contain the patient's experience of conversations between the patient and deceased, with the deceased clearly in control. The conversations are sometimes described as being in words, but at other times they are described as being "not in words" or telepathic; the meaning is communicated through a nonverbal understanding.

Anthony's Case: "Forgive and help your sister."

Anthony's mother had died three months before his session with me. A few days before her death, Anthony had been hospitalized in a distant part of the country because of recurring problems stemming from his post-traumatic stress disorder. He had been traumatized in childhood and occasionally the symptoms became so debilitating that he had to be admitted to a hospital until they subsided.

Because his post-traumatic stress disorder was worrisome to his mother, he didn't tell her or other family members he was being admitted again. No one knew where he was, so they couldn't locate him to tell him his mother had suddenly fallen gravely ill. When he learned of her illness, he returned home immediately, but his mother had already died.

Anthony experienced intense feelings of sadness and deep guilt that he couldn't be with his mother during her last few days. To make matters worse, in an outburst at the funeral home, his older sister loudly blamed him for their mother's death because she believed Anthony's post-traumatic stress disorder and his repeated hospitalizations so disturbed her that the stress eventually killed her. In despair and believing his sister was right, Anthony began psychotherapy to reduce the feelings of intense guilt and sadness.

I suggested to him that EMDR would help him resolve some of these feelings and that I would be using an additional component in the therapy that might help him understand his relationship with his mother.

I began with the standard core-focused EMDR process while he focused on his sadness. As his sadness increased, I repeated the eye movements until the sadness had peaked. When it seemed to be going down, I administered a set of eye movements, asked him to close his eyes, and told him to "Just let anything come to you naturally."

Anthony sat with his eyes closed for a minute, then opened them. "I saw my mother clearly. She was healthy and looked very peaceful. She . . . I can't say 'told' me, but I felt she said, without me hearing words, 'I love you, Tony, and I'm still with you in a very important way.' Then she said, 'You don't need to feel guilty. Your sister had some real difficulties and wasn't able to understand them. What she said to you came from her own problems, not anything having to do with you.'"

Anthony paused and said, "You can't imagine how good that made me feel. It seemed like it was really her talking to me. I said to her, 'What should I do, then?' She said, 'Forgive and help your sister.' I never figured I'd think of doing that."

Anthony's feelings of sadness and guilt fully resolved. That evening he called his sister, with whom he hadn't spoken since the funeral, and made arrangements for a visit. Six months later, I spoke with Anthony over the phone. His issues regarding his mother's death continued to be resolved, and he and his sister had been able to "patch things up." He explained that his sister confided that her anger toward him had been due to her own difficulty in dealing with the pain of her loss.

IADCs Often Contain Pointed Messages and Advice

When the messages contain advice, it is usually very specific and exactly what the patient needs to hear. The messages often contain helpful information that the patient can use to live a fuller, happier life.

Wayne's Case: "He told me he has forgiven the guy that killed him and I should forgive him too."

Wayne came to me because he had recurring, intrusive feelings of guilt about an incident that happened in Vietnam during his tour. Wayne had developed a close relationship with a soldier who came from the same town in Pennsylvania where he had grown up, although he hadn't known him before meeting him in Vietnam. They spent time together sharing stories about familiar places in the town and could often be heard laughing loudly about oddities in the little mill town they both knew so well.

One day on a mission to find a sniper they knew was in the wooded area close to the barracks, Wayne, his friend, and another soldier were walking through dense vegetation when they heard a sound. Wayne motioned to the other two soldiers to go forward and right while he circled left. A few minutes later, a shot rang out and Wayne heard his friend call, "Wayne, I'm hit." He ran over to where his friend lay, now dead from a mortal chest wound. The other soldier walked out from the foliage and, seeing the dead man, said, "I didn't know it was him. I just saw something move and fired." He had killed Wayne's friend accidentally.

Wayne was enraged and told the soldier to leave them; he'd take care of his friend. He brought his lifeless body back to camp.

The next day, Wayne and the soldier who had killed his friend were out searching for the same sniper. From the undergrowth, the sniper's bullet tore into the soldier's neck. Wayne saw the sniper and immediately shot him. Then he fell to his knees and held the soldier in his arms, looking at the wound. It was obviously fatal.

The soldier asked Wayne to forgive him for killing his friend. Wayne said he forgave him, but didn't mean it. He was still angry with the soldier for accidentally killing his friend. The soldier died in his arms.

Wayne finished telling me the story and said, "Dr. Al, I didn't really forgive him. I was still mad. I just said I forgave him 'cause I knew he was dying."

I asked Wayne to let himself feel his sadness for his friend while I administered a set of eye movements. His sadness increased and tears welled up from his eyes onto his cheeks. I did several sets of eye movements using the core-focused EMDR process. Finally, his sadness had increased to the point that he was unable to speak easily.

"How sad are you feeling now?" I asked.

"About a 10," he replied, referring to the 10-point scale we had been using to talk about the sadness.

"OK, stay with that feeling and let's do the eye movements again." After more eye movements, his sadness started to decrease. I did one more set and told him, "Stay with that feeling and when you close your eyes, let whatever comes just come."

He closed his eyes and sat quietly. After a few seconds, he opened his eyes and spoke. "I saw my friend from Pennsylvania. I saw him smiling at me. He looked real happy in a peaceful kind of way.

"He told me he has forgiven the guy that killed him because it was only a mistake. He said I should forgive him too." Wayne nodded his head slowly and looked at me intently. "You know, I can't explain it, but I suddenly feel like I've forgiven that guy for the first time in my life. How can that be? I've hated him every day for 28 years."

Wayne said he felt lighter after the session, like a huge burden had been lifted from him. Two weeks later, he met me, smiling and relieved. He immediately said, "I still feel like I've forgiven the guy and I don't feel bad about it at all. It's just like it's something that happened and it's over."

Truman's Case: Some stern advice—
"Stay out of other people's business."

Truman's case illustrates the insights a patient may receive during the IADC.

Truman's mother had died of cancer of the pancreas six years before he came to see me to help him with the intrusive memories of seeing her dead body in the hospital. When the doctor pronounced her dead, Truman hugged and kissed the body. The result was intrusive images of seeing her dead and feeling her lifeless body.

I had him focus on the distressing image first. I wanted to reduce the intensity of the image so he could go to the sadness he was feeling in core-focused EMDR. The image rapidly faded. Then I did core-focused EMDR to help him uncover the sadness. It increased in intensity until he was sobbing. After another set of eye movements, he said that it was getting better, so I helped him relax and become receptive to anything that might occur. Following two more sets of eye movements, the IADC began.

After he opened his eyes, he explained that his mother came to him looking many years younger than she had been when she died. She told him she was OK and that she still loved him. Truman sighed and smiled. "I feel she is fine now."

Then he explained that his mother gave him some stern advice. "Stay out of other people's business," he reported her saying. He said he knew immediately what she meant because he had recently been haranguing his old friend about the friend's wife's spending habits. It had caused a rift between his friend and him.

"I suppose she's right," he said. Six months later, he reported that he had let go of the issue from that day and felt better for having done so. His relationship with his friend had improved and his friend, seeing that Truman was no longer judging him, even made lighthearted jokes himself from time to time about his wife's spending behavior.

Don's Case: "Lennie was right. It's not right to not love my daughter the same way I loved him."

Don's case is another example of the wise advice patients report receiving from the deceased.

Don and his wife had very reluctantly agreed to allow their 12-year-old son, Lennie, to spend the summer out of state with cousins. They were very protective of Lennie, fearing that something might happen to him. Lennie was Don's "best buddy," and he was tearful as he watched Lennie board the plane.

Lennie had been with his cousins for two weeks when Don received the worst phone call a parent can receive. His son had been hit and killed by a car while walking on a dark country road. The incident devastated

Don. He had to identify his son's body lying on a slab in the morgue. The image of his son's fractured, white body had haunted him for the eight years before he came to see me. As often happens when a child dies, Don's marriage had broken up because of the stress. Don eventually remarried and had a daughter, but he was not able to feel close to her because of his unresolved grief over his son. Don cried as he told me his story.

I induced an IADC after two attempts and Don reported that he saw his son. He said his son was "very alive and very happy." He said he was wearing the same kind of clothes he liked to wear when alive. His son then told him that he loved him, and that it is OK to love other people and to get on with his life.

Don explained that his grief immediately and completely went away. He was shocked by his experience and said, "I know that was really him, I'm sure of it." He then said somberly, "You know, Lennie was right. It's not right to not love my daughter the same way I loved him. I'm committed to opening up emotionally with my daughter." He also said that the wonderful image he had of his son in the IADC had replaced the image of his body lying in the morgue.

I saw Don five months later. He said that his grief remained resolved and his relationship with his daughter had improved significantly.

Tyrone's Case: "You need to get on with your life and let this stuff go."

Tyrone was seeing me because of his combat trauma, but during the second session a more troubling sadness came up in our conversation. His brother had been murdered five years earlier. Tyrone felt strong rage toward the man he thought had murdered his brother. Although he had no proof that this man was the murderer, he often planned how he would kill the man to have his revenge.

In our session, he agreed to focus on his brother and we went through the IADC induction process. We first used EMDR to reduce the anger so the sadness could come through. When I began the core-focused EMDR, his sadness increased and he began to weep. He said he had tension in his stomach and I did a set of eye movements focusing on relaxing the tension. Then I told him to think about his brother and let whatever came, happen. When no IADC resulted, I repeated the procedure.

After the second induction, he sat quietly for a few minutes with his eyes closed. Then he opened his eyes and described what he saw. "I saw my brother's smiling face. He said, 'You need to get on with your life and let this stuff go.'"

Tyrone looked at me with a serious expression. "I know it was him," he said, "and I wouldn't accept that from anyone but him. I guess he's right."

The session ended and I didn't see Tyrone for a month. When I saw him again, he said he had stopped being angry the day of the session because he was going to get on with his life just as his brother told him he should. He was absolutely convinced that he had communicated with his deceased brother and it had changed his life.

Max's Case: "He had a higher calling, to be with the ones who really love him."

Being reunited with a loved one who has been missing for years is a joyous, life-changing experience for both people. The moment marks the beginning of new lives that will be fuller than they were, changed through the emotional reunion they experience.

That joy can be extinguished, however, when someone finally locates the long-lost child, parent, or sibling, and learns the loved one has passed away. The reunion will never happen. All of the days they could have spent together, answers to questions about each other's lives, and memories they could have shared evaporate in death. With IADC therapy, however, that sense of being reunited can still heal the patient's grief even though the loved one has died.

That is what Max learned. In the process, he also demonstrated a characteristic common to IADCs. Often the experience not only resolves grief, but also provides the patient with a profoundly positive insight.

Max came to my office because of his overwhelming feelings of guilt and sadness. He had married more than 23 years before, but the marriage had been brief, failing after a short time. His wife left him, taking their infant son across the country and remarrying. Since Max was not in the child's life and her new husband wanted to become the child's father, she asked Max to give up all custody rights and allow her new husband to adopt the child. "It was the hardest decision of my life," he said, "but I wanted my son to have a stable home life, so I signed the papers."

Max eventually remarried, but never fathered any more children. His new wife had children, but he didn't feel like a father to them. He kept hoping that someday he would find his biological son and develop a relationship.

One day, Max answered the phone and heard the caller say, "You haven't seen me for a long time. I'm your son." Max's spirits soared as he listened to his son talk about his life. He said he and his mother, Max's ex-wife, weren't getting along and he wanted to leave home. He said he had always dreamed of living with his biological dad.

Max was elated. His life's dream was coming true. As soon as he hung up the phone, Max began planning how the two could meet and talk about arranging for his son to live with him. But when he called to finalize the arrangements, he learned that his son had committed suicide. Max was crushed; the hope that had sustained him for 18 years had died with his son.

Now, four years later, Max had come for therapy to try to reduce the despondence that dominated his life. I used core-focused EMDR to get in touch with his sadness. When the sadness started to diminish, I began the induction.

Max closed his eyes and almost immediately started describing what he was seeing. "I can see my son and my dad fishing together in the most beautiful place I have ever seen," he said. "Dad has been dead for years. My son is asking Dad questions about me. Dad is telling him stories about me when I was growing up."

He opened his eyes and said, "I think I know now why my son died. He had a higher calling, to be with the ones who really love him." He thought for a minute. "You know, I used to feel like I had been cheated because I didn't have my own son with me. But now I feel like I can give all my love to my stepchildren, just as Dad is giving his love to my son. I need to be more giving and less selfish."

Max opened a new door in his life and walked through it confidently and happily. He had felt a reconnection with his son in a way that changed his connections with those who were still alive. The IADC therapy experience changed him from feeling cheated to feeling enriched.

Patients Sometimes Perceive the Deceased Asking Them to Relay Messages to Living Relatives

We have a number of cases in which the patient has reported the deceased wanting the patient to relay messages to family members. Butch's IADC contains an example of such a request.

Butch's Case: "Look after my wife and daughter."

Butch and his closest friend in Vietnam, Tom, became separated in the confusion of their unit's worst battle. When it was over, he discovered that Tom had been killed, but he never found out exactly what had happened. He cried as he put Tom's body on a helicopter. They had trained together in the States, took all of their leave time together, and had even made plans to go into business together after the war. As Butch explained his story to me, he wept with his face in his hands.

After three IADC inductions, Butch closed his eyes and saw Tom standing before him. He reported what he experienced with his eyes still closed: "Tom looks healthy and very happy. He just explained what happened. He said 'I got caught out in the open and wasn't watching, so I paid the price. But now I'm still with you and watching out for you.'" Butch reported that Tom then said, "Look after my wife and daughter."

Butch opened his eyes at that point, looking perplexed. He said he was in no position to help Tom's wife and daughter because they lived a great distance from him. "Even if they were here," he continued, "I don't have enough money to make it myself. I couldn't help them right now."

I told Butch to keep that issue in mind and go back. I administered a set of eye movements and he closed his eyes. With his eyes still closed, Butch described what he experienced. "Tom says he meant that he wants me to talk to his wife and daughter, and especially his daughter. He says she was born right after he was killed and she often wonders about him and what kind of person he was."

Butch opened his eyes, visibly moved by the request. "Tom said he wants me to tell his daughter all about him. I'm going to find her and do it."

All of Butch's issues related to Tom's death were resolved and he made plans to try to locate his friend's wife and daughter.

Every IADC Thus Far Has Been Positive, None Negative

Some NDEs described in the literature have negative content. In the more than three thousand IADCs we have induced thus far, however, not one has contained negative content. If a patient reports a negative impression during an IADC, we always learn, by going back into the IADC experience, that it was the result of intrusive memories or a misinterpreted IADC, not the IADC itself.

Even when the experiencer goes into the induction process with fear about confronting the deceased because of abuse and trauma, the experiencer always, without exception, perceives the deceased as being loving, remorseful or forgiving, attentive, and compassionate. In no instance has the experiencer described an angry, blaming, or harsh message from the deceased. Messages are always loving, insightful, and uplifting.

For example, I was very amused by the experience a patient named Dan had when he attempted to have an IADC focusing on his deceased older brother. After the normal core-focused EMDR and IADC induction procedure, Dan closed his eyes thinking about his brother, then suddenly opened them with a start. He blurted out, with his eyes wide, "I felt huge claws clamping around me."

I said, "Dan, these experiences have so far always been positive. Go back to it and find out what happened."

Trusting me, he agreed to go back to the IADC, focusing on his brother again. I administered another set of eye movements and he closed his eyes. In a moment, he smiled. After a few seconds, he opened his eyes. "I saw my brother this time. It was just like we were together before he died and I felt I could just talk to him. I asked him if he knew what the claw thing was. He said it wasn't a claw. He was just giving me a big hug. He hugged me again and I could feel it. My brother's OK."

The Experience May Be with One Person, Several, or an Entire Group

The reconnection scenarios the patients describe may involve one person, two or three people, or even a group of deceased people. Often, deceased people other than the one who is the focus of the survivor's grief appear in the IADC. At times, an entire group can appear, particularly when the deceased members of that group were known to each other.

Paul's Case: "All the guys in the company who had died were waving."

Paul had finally made it out of Vietnam after 12 months. The war was over for him. But soon after getting home, he learned that most of his company had been killed a few days after he left, including Larry, his best friend. The news was devastating. He had left the war, but it hadn't left him. For the next 29 years, he kept seeing images of what it must have been like when they were all killed. And the memories of his friend and the plans they had made to meet and have fun together when they were both in the States created unbearable bouts of sadness.

He came to me to see whether I could help him resolve some of the grief. We decided to focus on Larry. I did the eye movements to get him in touch with the core sadness, and when it peaked and started back down, I went through two IADC induction procedures.

On the second induction, Paul sat quietly, then opened his eyes and reported what had happened. "Larry was standing in front of me. I could actually see him. But here's the really strange thing. Behind him, I could see a crowd of guys standing like they were on bleachers. It was all the guys in the company who had died, about a hundred of them, and they were waving at me. I looked down the rows and I was going, 'There's Frank and I remember the guy next to him but don't know his name. I don't know the guy beside him, but Lou's behind him.' They were all there. I hadn't thought about them for 29 years. I'll tell you what it looked like. It was like an old photograph of a team, but they were all moving and waving. They all showed up for me."

Boris's Case: "They're all saluting me."

Boris came to me because he was having intrusive memories of his shipmates, dead and dying after an explosion. He had been in the navy on a carrier in WWII. One day, a fire started and spread rapidly, reaching the boilers. When they blew up, the explosion ignited jet fuel and a tremendous explosion killed 28 sailors. He was one of those charged with removing the bodies. The charred corpses and body parts caused intrusive memories that stayed with him for the next 55 years.

I listened to his tragic story, unable to fully comprehend the misery he must have been experiencing every day of his life after the war. He agreed to allow me to use EMDR to get in touch with the sadness and induce an IADC. After a few sets of eye movements, his sadness peaked and was coming back down. I did two more sets of eye movements. "Think about the sailors who died that day in a general way," I told him on the third induction, "and just be open to anything that happens." He closed his eyes and the IADC began.

"I can see all 28 of them. They're in their dress blues. I can't believe it." He smiled. The tears had stopped and he was deep into the scene being played out behind his closed eyes. He shook his head slowly.

"What do you see?"

"They're all saluting me. They're giving me the feeling it's OK. They look happy and at peace."

The intrusive memories did not return after that day. Instead, he enjoyed talking about the sailors he knew who had died, and referred to them individually as they had appeared in his IADC.

Betty's Case: "Tell my daughter I'm OK."

Betty had a very close relationship with Hank, her father-in-law, before he died. She described him as "a very gentle man with a heart of gold." After he retired, Hank would come daily to Betty's house to care for her two sons, his grandchildren, so Betty and her husband could pursue their professional careers. When Hank suddenly died of a heart attack, Betty and her husband were devastated.

About three years later, Betty came to me for psychotherapy involving a problem not related to Hank. When the subject of her father-in-law's death came up during the course of therapy, it was clear that she had residual sadness. I explained IADCs and asked her whether she would like to participate in one to resolve her feelings about Hank's death. She laughed and said, "It won't work with me. I'm much better with his death now and, besides, I don't believe in that kind of stuff anyway." Betty nevertheless was willing to give it a try.

Her sadness was not overwhelming, but it increased somewhat with a set of eye movements. The next set brought it down and I began the induction. Betty closed her eyes and almost immediately said, "I can see him. . . . It's Hank. He looks 20 years younger than when he died." She paused. "He's thoroughly at peace, and completely happy."

She paused again for a few seconds, then opened her eyes. "He told me he is very proud of me and my husband. But you know something really interesting happened then. Hank's sister appeared. She died about seven years before Hank, I think. She said, 'Tell my daughter I'm OK.'"

Betty then told me that not only was she surprised at the communication with her father-in-law, she was very confused by the fact that Hank's sister had appeared during her IADC. Betty explained to me that she had met Hank's sister on one occasion at a family reunion; she didn't know her well and didn't know her daughter at all.

Betty was euphoric and confused. She ended our session by saying, "I never would have believed it, but that was really Hank. I still don't know why his sister was there. I certainly didn't expect that. And how the hell am I going to tell her daughter that her mother's OK. She'll think I'm a total nut case. I didn't make this shit up, Doctor. It just happened."

Betty's case is common among people who have experienced IADCs. Her experience was not at all consistent with her beliefs and expectations. She was not only very surprised that she had an IADC, she was also startled by the appearance of Hank's sister, which she clearly believed was not of her making. It is not unusual for the patient to describe the deceased being with someone who was important to the deceased in life, but relatively unknown and unimportant to the patient.

The Personalities of the Deceased Come Out in the IADC

Patients often remark, "Yeah, that's just like him" or "She sure hasn't changed." Their perceptions of the reconnection describe the deceased with the same personality traits he or she displayed when alive.

Jarrod's Case: "You're late again. You're always showing up late."

Greg Rimoldi, one of the psychotherapists I trained in IADC therapy, was treating Jarrod for post-traumatic stress disorder resulting from his tour in Vietnam. One of the intrusive memories resulted from the deaths of most of the men in his unit in a firefight.

Jarrod said, "We knew they were out there and we were sent to the flank to try to get at them. Suddenly, we were attacked by a large group of VC [Vietcong]. We were calling in artillery fire right on top of us to try to get out of there alive. Everyone was killed but six or seven of us."

Greg did an IADC induction to help Jarrod with the intrusive memories, sadness, and guilt at surviving the firefight. After the last set of eye movements, the patient closed his eyes. He opened them a few minutes later, laughing.

He explained, "When I first saw them, it was like I was going up to them. They were all there. There were some corporals and sergeants in the group. They said to me, 'Oh yeah, you're late again. You're always showing up late.' They sure haven't changed."

Jarrod then said to Greg, "I thought there'd be something holy about this, with trumpets and angels. It wasn't. It was just like another day in Nam before the firefight. But it wasn't a memory. It never happened like that."

Patients Sometimes Perceive Messages They Don't Expect and Don't Want

One of the unusual characteristics of IADCs is that the patient often perceives messages that are completely unexpected or are actually what the patient would not want to hear.

Bill's Case: "Forgive Mom. It wasn't her fault and you should get back together."

Bill's son had been shot to death as a result of his gang-related activities about two years before our session. Bill said he viewed himself as a strict disciplinarian with his children. He believed his wife's overly lax approach was a major contributing factor in their son's death. Soon after the funeral, Bill moved out of the family home. For the next two years, he lived an isolated, lonely life.

As he told me his story, he alternated between intense anger and profound sadness at his loss. After core-focused EMDR, I initiated an IADC and he had one without difficulty. In it, Bill saw his son happy and peaceful. But he said his son was very concerned about the pain his family was experiencing over his premature and unexpected death.

Bill reported that his son told him no one should feel any anger or guilt because it was his choice to do what he did. He told Bill, however, that he realized he had made some bad decisions. His son then asked Bill to forgive his mother because it wasn't her fault and to try to work things out with her so they could get back together.

After the IADC, Bill reported that he felt connected to his son and he was no longer experiencing sadness. When I asked him what he thought about his son's advice to try to reconcile with his wife, he said emphatically, "No way." From that point on, Bill refused to examine his anger further.

Although Bill's overall psychological condition at the end of therapy was markedly improved, he did not exhibit the same overall dramatic changes others did who had experienced IADCs.

The advice Bill received from his son was not only unexpected, it was in direct conflict with what he was convinced was true: that his wife had been responsible for their son's death. This case also provides a good example of one of the few IADC induction sessions in which not all issues were resolved. I strongly suspect, however, that had Bill been willing to pursue the issue of his anger further, complete resolution would have occurred.

Patients Sometimes Report Seeing the Spirit of the Deceased Rise from the Body or Stand over the Body

Some patients experiencing an IADC describe the death scene and report seeing the spirit of the deceased rising from the body or standing over the body. This kind of experience most often occurs when the witness does not know the deceased personally. In all cases, these IADCs occur spontaneously after an induction and are not suggested to the patient.

Jason's experience is an example of seeing the deceased standing over his lifeless body.

Jason's Case: "It's better to die the first week in country than the last week. I got out of 12 more miserable months in Nam."

Jason had been a chopper pilot in Vietnam during the war. One day when he was scheduled to fly a routine mission, he was feeling very ill and asked a young chopper pilot new to the war to fly the mission for him. The young soldier was eager to prove his capability, so he happily agreed to take over the mission while Jason spent the day on his cot. That afternoon, Jason's commanding officer woke him to tell him that his chopper had crashed and burned. All on board were lost, including the substitute pilot.

The impact on Jason was crushing. He felt intense sadness and tremendous guilt that this young pilot had been killed. He believed that he was the one who should have died. The guilt and grief he felt for the young pilot remained intense over the years.

Jason told me the story sternly, but the quiver in his chin and stiff posture revealed that he was suppressing deep sadness and guilt. I asked him how he was feeling and he shrugged, unable to speak. Then said abruptly, "Fair," and looked away with a sigh. I explained EMDR to him and administered the first set of eye movements. After the eye movements, I told him to close his eyes and let the feelings come naturally. Tears rolled down his face.

"What are you feeling?" I asked.

He opened his eyes and spoke, "Not so good." He began to sob.

"Stay with that feeling and we'll do the eye movements again," I said.

We did another set of eye movements, then another, until it appeared that his sadness had reached a peak. Using core-focused EMDR, I knew we had uncovered the core sadness and I could help him through it if we stayed with the feeling. Many EMDR psychotherapists would stop at this point and have the patient imagine being in a "safe place" to reduce the patient's distress, but I knew that stopping the process would just leave the deeply seated emotional issues in place to haunt him.

I did another set of eye movements and he closed his eyes. Then it happened. He was openly crying when he first closed his eyes, but he suddenly stopped crying and craned his head forward as though looking and listening. After a minute of silence, he opened his eyes wide and looked at me. "I saw him," he said. "I saw that young guy. He was standing over his own body feeling real worried about how his family back home was going to take it."

He turned his face away for a moment, remembering, then looked at me. "I could see his body. It was mangled and burned, but there he was, just as real as you or me, standing perfectly healthy, looking at it. Then the guy looked at me. He said, 'It's not at all your fault. I wanted to make that flight. You shouldn't feel responsible. I'm OK with that.'" Jason's frame relaxed and he was smiling.

"Just let whatever happens happen," I said, and directed more eye movements.

He closed his eyes, sat motionless for a moment, then smiled and opened his eyes. "This time I saw just the guy. He was looking at me and I could tell what he was saying, but I didn't hear words. He said his family is doing fine. His wife has remarried and he's happy about that." He laughed. "He even made a joke. He said, 'It's better to die the first week in country than the last week.' He said, 'I got out of 12 more miserable months in Nam.'"

At the end of the session, Jason shook my hand vigorously and walked out of my office, smiling.

Patients Sometimes Feel a Love That Was Not Freely Given in Life

Some of the people who came to me for therapy describe relationships with deceased loved ones that were emotionally empty. Their loved ones were distant, harsh, or unavailable. As a result, they didn't experience the reassurance that they were loved. After the loved one's death, it seems to them that they will never experience the love they so desperately wanted. Some of the IADC experiences, however, provide the sense that the love they wanted is there.

Bruce's Case: "I know now that I have been lonely because I felt I could never have a lasting love with someone."

Bruce was one of the veterans I treated for post-traumatic stress disorder. In the course of treatment, he confided to me that he had always felt lonely and couldn't understand why.

I asked him about his childhood and he explained that his biological father had left him and his mother when he was only three years old. His mother remarried and Bruce had a stepfather who was everything a father could be, but Bruce never felt loved and accepted by his stepfather. He felt his stepfather loved his biological son, Bruce's half brother, more.

From the time his biological father left until he was a teenager, Bruce would hear from other family members about what his father was doing and he was very interested in his father, but never saw him again in his youth.

Bruce's biological father finally came to visit when Bruce was 32 years old, but it wasn't an uplifting experience. Bruce was in the process of breaking up with his wife and had some issues about his father's absence that he had harbored for years. When his father showed up out of the blue, Bruce wasn't receptive to him. His father talked entirely about himself during the visit, and though Bruce tried to listen politely, he was glad when the visit was over.

Years passed. Bruce was in his early fifties when he learned his biological father had died. For some reason he didn't understand, he went into deep sadness and a feeling of utter loneliness.

I described the IADC process to him and he agreed to give it a try. After three induction procedures, the IADC began. Bruce said he saw a man come out of an arch of bright, pure white light. As the man came closer, he could see his face. He thought, "That looks just like my father," but he said the man appeared younger than his father had looked the one time he met with him, more like the pictures he had seen of his father taken when his father was a young man.

But he said he knew it was his father when the man said, "I'm sorry. Everything is going to be OK." After a few seconds, he experienced his father walking back through the arch and disappearing.

"That was really my father. I'm sure of it," he said. "It was him."

Bruce still had sadness in his face, so I asked what the sadness was from. He answered, "I still feel like something is missing."

"What's that?" I asked.

Tears formed in his eyes and rolled down his cheeks. "I miss my father's love."

I told him to keep that in mind and induced another IADC. He closed his eyes and almost immediately burst into tears. After a few seconds, he opened his eyes.

"I didn't see my father this time," he said, "but I felt his love. When I felt that, it made me think of something I hadn't thought of in 49 years. I had forgotten what my father's love was, but I remember being held by my father when I was little."

The memories began to reform and he explained what he was feeling. He had been around three when he experienced his father's love for him. Then one day, it was gone, when his father left, never to come back. There were moments in his life when he had felt lonely, but he had always attributed them to things going on in his life. Now he understood where that loneliness came from. He also understood why he never felt loved by his stepfather.

A week before this session, he had walked out on his girlfriend because he felt she was rejecting him; in this, he was playing out the script that told him he should be alone in his life.

"I know now that it was because I felt I could never have a lasting love with someone," explained Bruce. "Anyone I loved would end up leaving and taking the love away again."

As the session ended, he said he understood that much of his loneliness had nothing to do with the current situation; it resulted from the loss of love and his longing to experience it again. He added that he planned to reconcile with his girlfriend. At his next session, he reported that for the last week, he "felt whole for the first time in many years" and that he had renewed his relationship with his girlfriend.

Kathy's Case: "Dad, I forgive you for the problems we had. I really always loved you and I love you now."

Kathy's mother had died when she was 12 years old. She had maintained a satisfactory relationship with her father until he remarried three years later. "After that," she said, "he became cold and distant, not just to me but to everyone. He never had anything positive to say to anyone."

Kathy explained that she had responded to her mother's death and the intrusion of a stepmother with rebellious, acting-out behavior that created problems for her at home and at school. Her father became more authoritarian, tightening control over her. She rebelled even more strenuously and their relationship deteriorated to the point that they hardly spoke; when they did, it was often in anger.

In the 24 years since she had left home, her relationship with her father had been strained. As she described it, "The relationship never fully recovered from the problems we had after Mom's death."

Three months before she came to see me, her father had died, leaving her sad and empty.

I felt that an IADC induction would help her with her feelings. When I described the IADC procedure, she said she thought it sounded "weird," but was willing to give it a try. I began the induction process and, after her sadness peaked and started going down, I provided a set of eye movements and told her to think about her father in a general way and go with whatever happened. She closed her eyes and after a minute opened them with a frown. "I just could see him in the casket. What was that supposed to do for me?"

I did another set of eye movements asking her to picture her father lying in the casket. She reported that the image faded. I gave her more eye movements and instructed her to think about her father and just be open to anything that happened. She closed her eyes and sat quietly for a couple of minutes.

After she opened her eyes, she said, "I saw him sitting in a brightly lit, beautiful, rich green field. I said to him, 'I've been screwed up my whole life because of the way you treated me.' He was looking at me and seemed to be paying very close attention to what I was saying. I asked him, 'Why?' I could sense him saying to me, 'I didn't know what else to do. You wouldn't listen, and I didn't know how to reach you.'"

Kathy said her father sounded very loving and compassionate, in a tone she had never experienced before. She told me that she fully experienced her father's love for her. "My father said he was proud of some recent changes that I had made in my life. I said, 'Dad, I forgive you for the problems we had. I really always loved you and I love you now.'" She smiled, in tears.

"After that," she said, "his image faded. But you know, right now I don't feel angry with him, and I don't feel as awful about his death. I know that was real; there is no way I could have thought that up. It was kind of strange, because it was like he could talk to me through my mind with feelings."

Her anger and grief remained resolved in the months that followed.

Reconnecting with a Loved One Who Has Committed Suicide Helps the Grieving Process

One of the prominent, recurring lessons we have learned from both IADCs and NDEs is that when someone has caused pain to others in life, the person doesn't get away with it. In the life review portion of the NDE, the experiencer faces the emotional effects of his or her actions on others. In IADCs, the deceased who committed suicide is experienced as aware of the pain the suicide caused to friends and loved ones. The result is deep remorse in every IADC on the part of the person who committed suicide, with the common message being: "I'm really sorry. I really didn't know my suicide would have this effect on everyone. It wasn't your fault." The IADC helps to heal the special grief that survivors of a suicide feel.

In cases of suicide, especially suicide by children, there is an even more important reason to induce an IADC. For parents of children who have committed suicide, working through the loss is frequently complicated by issues of unfinished business. The unfinished business in these cases is not only a critical matter for survivors, it is generally experienced in IADCs as critical for the deceased.

Bob's Case: "Dad, I should have listened to you. It was my fault, not yours. Please forgive me."

A year before Bob came to see me, his daughter had committed suicide. Every day of that year, he replayed his self-indictment that he had not done enough for her, that he could have prevented her from killing herself if he had just been different, and that her suicide was his fault. Every day, he eventually broke down in tears, mentally and emotionally exhausted from turning the thoughts over in his mind. He was unable to focus on his job, and the weekly grief support group didn't diminish his torment.

He cried as he sat in my office. "I thought I was a good father, but obviously I wasn't," he said.

We went through the usual core-focused EMDR, and his sadness became intense for a few minutes before decreasing. I asked him what he would want to say to his daughter. He said, "I'm sorry, I'm so sorry."

I then induced the IADC. Bob sat for a minute with his eyes closed, moving his head slightly from side to side. A nod indicated to me that he was likely experiencing an IADC. A slight smile crept across his face.

Bob opened his eyes and told me what had happened. "As soon as I closed my eyes, Jane appeared to me, and started talking right away. She looked wonderful. She said she was very worried about me, that she was lucky to have a father like me, and that it wasn't my fault. Then she said that she had not understood what real love is, and that she had been despondent because of her breakup with Jake, her boyfriend. Then she said to me, 'Dad, I should have listened to you. It was my fault, not yours. Please forgive me.'"

"I said, 'I forgive you, honey.'"

Bob smiled warmly, "She gave me a hug and said, 'I'm OK now, and I want you to be OK too—I want you to know that I am still and will always be with you, Daddy-do.' She used to call me that when she sat on my lap when she was very little. That made me feel happy."

As with all IADCs, Bob's experience of reconnection with his daughter did much to reduce his sadness and guilt. Bob called me two years after our session and reported that he was still doing much better, and he believed his daughter was with him in a very important way.

Pets Sometimes Appear in IADCs

In some of the IADCs, deceased pets appear. Patients report that the pets recognize them and come to them excitedly as they did when they were alive.

Phil's Case: "They're wagging their tails and coming up to me, just like they did in Nam."

While serving in Vietnam during the war, Phil was awakened one evening by the sound of whimpering outside the barracks. He recognized it as a dog's cry because he had grown up with dogs. He walked out of the barracks and found a stray black-and-white female dog, thin, mangy, and looking at him sorrowfully. He brought her into the barracks and gave her some of his rations.

Over several weeks, he nursed her to health and looked forward to seeing her each day when he returned from patrol. He named her Mollie after the dog he had loved as a child and remembered most. He wondered why, when her body was malnourished and thin, her belly was so plump. One morning he found out why; she had given birth to three puppies. He cared for the puppies and Mollie with great love, little reminders of his home and childhood.

Then one day, orders came down that stray dogs had become a nuisance in the camp and all were to be killed. Phil was distraught. He took Mollie and her puppies outside of the base camp and hid them in an improvised shelter. Over the next few days, he sneaked outside the camp daily to give them food and water. An officer found out about his dogs, however, and told Phil either he would have to kill them or the officer would. Without an alternative, Phil said he would prefer to kill them. That afternoon, he tearfully shot Mollie and her three puppies.

He finished the story in my office crying uncontrollably. It was one of the most traumatic memories he had brought with him from Vietnam.

I did core-focused EMDR with him, combining his sadness with the image of killing Mollie and the puppies. His sadness increased, then began to soften. On the third IADC induction, with his eyes closed, he described what he saw.

"I can see Mollie," he began, "and her three puppies. They're wagging their tails and coming up to me, just like they did in Nam." He paused, smiling. "They're jumping around and coming up on me. I feel like I'm sitting on the ground." He was still for a moment, then started laughing. He opened his eyes. "That was wonderful, Dr. Al," he said, beaming. "Mollie and the puppies were with me. Then I saw another dog coming to me. It was the Mollie I had when I was growing up, the one I named my Vietnam Mollie after. She jumped on me and was licking me. Then there were more. All the dogs I had as a kid came to me and were jumping on me and licking me like they missed me and were happy to see me."

Phil reported two months later that all his grief and traumatic memories of Mollie's death had disappeared, and when he imagined them, he saw only the two Mollies and puppies playing together happily.

Melinda's Case: "I said 'Sit,' and they stopped jumping on me."

In another IADC containing pets, the pets responded to commands.

Melinda's Uncle Darren had been like a father to her. He lived not far from her home and when her parents were working evenings at the family restaurant, Melinda would stay with her aunt and uncle. She especially liked playing with Uncle Darren's two dogs, Paris and Rinnie. They were large dogs, one a border collie and the other a German shepherd. "They would give me doggie hugs when they stood on their hind legs to lick my face," she said. "They died while I was a teenager and I really miss them."

Three weeks before she came to me, her Uncle Darren had passed away from a heart attack. She was in grief over her uncle's death and wept as she described warm memories of her uncle and his love for her.

When she was ready, I went through the normal core-focused EMDR process and when her sadness started to come down, I gave her a set of eye movements and told her, "Think about your uncle again and close your eyes. Let whatever happens come naturally."

She closed her eyes and almost immediately opened them, lurching forward in her chair. "Something jumped on me," she blurted with her eyes open wide. "I don't know what it was."

"Melinda," I said, "IADCs are always positive. There's nothing to be afraid of. If you go back to it, you probably will understand what is happening, whatever that is." She looked at me out of the corner of her eye. "OK, I'll do it, but if it happens again, that's it for this stuff."

I provided another set of eye movements and Melinda, a little tense, closed her eyes. After a few seconds, she relaxed, smiled, and shook her head. She opened her eyes.

"I saw my uncle very clearly," she said. He was holding Paris and Rinnie on leashes. They were straining to come to me and wagging their tails. He said he loves me and will always be with me."

Melinda was overjoyed about her experience and felt sure her uncle was still alive with Paris and Rinnie, just in a different form. She left my office happy, without the feelings of grief she had when she came to me.

The next day, I was surprised to see Melinda at my office door. "Dr. Botkin, can I talk to you for a minute?" She was obviously upset, which surprised me after her positive IADC experience.

"Sure," I said. "Come in and sit down."

She sat slowly with her brow furrowed. "Last night I had these really strange sensations; I felt things jumping on me again just like yesterday when you first did the IADC with me. I don't want that to happen again. What do you think this is?"

I suspected what it was, but didn't tell her. "Let's do another IADC and maybe your uncle can help you understand," I said. She agreed and we went through the induction process. She closed her eyes and, after a moment, a smile lit up her face. "Paris and Rinnie," she said softly, nodding her head. "It was Paris and Rinnie."

She opened her eyes. "I saw Uncle Darren again. He had Paris and Rinnie. He let them go and they jumped up on me and were licking my face. That's exactly what I felt last night. I looked over at Uncle Darren and could tell he was saying to me, 'Paris and Rinnie want you to know they're all right too.'"

"That's not the best part. They were jumping all over me and licking my face, so we played for a minute. Then I did what I used to do when they were alive. I said 'Sit,' and they stopped jumping on me. They just sat looking up at me with their tails wagging."

I spoke with Melinda two months later. She reported that she had experienced no further incidents of the sensation that something was jumping on her. She was sure it was because she had told Paris and Rinnie to sit and they were still obeying.

Craig's Case: "I felt soft fur against my cheek and heard her purr."

Craig, the coauthor of this book, has always loved animals, from the wildlife he photographs to the Akita and border collie he rescued. He was delighted one winter day to discover that a wild cat had given birth to a litter under his expansive front porch. Three little gray heads and one set of tiger-striped ears would appear through holes in the brickwork and then draw back timidly. After weeks of coaxing them with food, he finally was able to touch them, then pet them, and finally hold them.

The striped kitty, christened Tiger, would look into his eyes as he fed the four kittens chicken scraps to entice them onto his lap. Tiger's brother and two sisters would allow only Craig to come near them. He had them neutered, put collars on them with ID tags, and for months enjoyed having them come into his office, softly walk onto his chest as he sat in his recliner reading, and purr themselves to sleep.

Because they were still essentially feral, the kittens were allowed to come and go freely through a special kitten-sized door. One day, Craig received a phone call from the local animal control telling him that they had Tiger's ID tag. She had been hit by a car and killed. His sadness over her death showed him how attached he had grown to the kittens.

A week later, we were discussing pet IADCs in a gathering of psychotherapists who had been trained in the procedure. Craig suggested that I do an IADC on him with Tiger as his focus. I agreed and we went through the induction process.

This is what he experienced when he closed his eyes: "Almost immediately, I could feel gentle touches on my chest. I leaned back in response. Then I felt soft fur against my cheek and heard purring. The sensations were unmistakable. After a few seconds, the sensations stopped and I opened my eyes. I was sure that it was little Tiger visiting me to tell me she is still with me and her brother and sisters."

Senses, Hugs, Healthy Vibrant People, and Beautiful Landscapes

Some IADCs are visual, some auditory, some tactile, a few olfactory, and most have some combination of the senses. Touches and hugs are relatively common. Some experiencers describe having only a "knowing," with no sensory experience. When the patient expects or wants the IADC experience in one mode, such as sight, it often comes in another mode. An expectation for any mode apparently blocks the IADC in that mode because patients are trying too hard in that mode.

People who were very old or ill before death are always experienced as younger and healthier. Children who die are sometimes experienced as still young and sometimes as older.

Beautiful landscapes are common in IADCs, with picturesque trees, green hills, flowering bushes, lush expanses of grass, shimmering lakes, and streams. Patients typically describe colors as being brighter and richer than normal; sometimes they use words such as "radiant" or "iridescent." They often describe the environment as exuding peace and serenity.

Sometimes people with expectations based on their religious beliefs are surprised by the familiar but richer earthly environments in their IADC experiences. Interestingly, although most of my patients have a background in Christianity and are steeped in the common traditions of what an afterlife is like, no patient has described a hell, trumpets, angels, pearly gates, or any other of the typical images commonly appearing in afterlife descriptions.

Early in my exploration of the IADC phenomenon, I drew additional generalizations from sessions with the first 84 patients to help me understand the phenomenon (see appendix C). Because every IADC is unique and neither the therapist nor the patient has control over the experience, nearly all IADCs are experienced as surprising and inconsistent with expectations. Some are so extraordinary, however, that I present them separately in the next chapter to illustrate some of the more unusual content that can arise during an IADC.

6

Extraordinary IADC Cases

A miracle is not the breaking of physical laws, but rather represents laws which are incomprehensible to us.

—G. I. Gurdjieff

My psychotherapist colleagues and I who have been doing IADCs for eight years occasionally share the content of sessions to compare notes about methods. We also describe what we are discovering. Sometimes we are awestruck by an experience and need to talk with another psychotherapist about it.

At first, every IADC was a remarkable occurrence and we were always on the phone or striding into a colleague's office to describe excitedly what had happened. After all, the IADC experience is unplanned, unguided, and unpredictable. After the therapist prepares the patient to be open and receptive, nothing about the content of the experience can be directed or controlled by either the patient or the therapist.

Among these unusual IADCs are some so extraordinary in their poignancy, drama, or sensory content that after we describe them, we just look at each other in silence. The previous chapter contained IADCs we have seen commonly in our practices. This chapter contains unusual cases that happen rarely; as such, they are different from the other IADCs in this book, but I have included them because they further our understanding of IADCs.

IADC Experiences in Which Living People Appeared

IADCs heal grief by allowing patients to feel they are connecting with someone who has passed away. In no instances other than the two cases that follow has a living person appeared in a patient's IADC. I present the cases here to provide additional perspectives on the IADC experience.

Jeff's Case: "Jason told me I shouldn't feel bad about his medical condition because it allows him to experience the best of both worlds."

Jeff's severely disabled 18-year-old son, Jason, had been diagnosed with microencephalopathy and had a mental age of only six months. Jeff told me he loved his son dearly and was very proud that Jason always "perked up" and became "very playful" when Jeff came home from work. Jeff came to see me to address psychological problems unrelated to his son and we successfully worked through his issues. The therapy included two successful IADCs. In one of his IADCs, a severely deformed friend who had died appeared as unimpaired and healthy. Seeing a parallel between his friend's condition and his son's, Jeff asked me if it would be possible to do an IADC focused on his severely retarded son.

I had, at that point, induced IADCs only to assist people in dealing with grief associated with death. In some of the cases, the patients' grief was resolved when they felt they had seen loved ones who were disabled or impaired in life appearing whole, healthy, and fully functioning in their IADC experience. I agreed to try it.

I performed the usual induction and Jeff closed his eyes. Nothing happened, so I repeated the induction process and he closed his eyes again. In a moment, he spoke: "I can see Jason surrounded by a beautiful radiant light. My God, he's talking." Jeff's son had never learned to talk because of his severe retardation. "He's thanking me for being such a wonderful father to him. He says 'I'm here to look after you.'" Jeff sat quietly with his eyes closed for a few minutes as tears rolled down his cheeks.

Then he opened his eyes and told me what had happened. "Jason told me I shouldn't feel bad about his medical condition because it allows him to experience both worlds at the same time."

As he was preparing to leave, Jeff said that the experience had made him feel more at peace with his son's condition. He also said he would never look at his son the same way again.

Ramona's Case: "Would you tell my mom I'm OK?"

One of the more unusual IADCs involved a patient experiencing the deceased trying to contact a relative. The patient's name was Ramona.

Ramona's older cousin had died of AIDS about six months before she came to see me. She described her cousin as "not a nice guy" when he was living. He was the neighborhood bully as a child and graduated to violent criminal behavior as an adult. He had been in and out of prison his whole life.

She was not sad over her cousin's death, but wanted to do an IADC with him as the subject because she had experienced a successful IADC before and wanted to see what insights she could have about him.

We went through the induction process three times and, on the fourth, Ramona closed her eyes, sat quietly, and after a minute, laughed. A few seconds later, she opened her eyes and explained what happened. "I saw my cousin standing in front of me. He said to me, 'I'm OK.' Then he said something that shook me up. He said, 'You have to take care of yourself.' I know he was talking about a physical problem I'm having. 'Or I'll pop you in the head.' He used to say that to me all the time when we were kids. I didn't remember that until he said it just now. But he said it as a joke now and I laughed. He laughed too."

She leaned forward and shook her head slowly. "Then something really creepy happened. I saw his mother kind of off a ways with her back to us and he was trying to tell his mother he is OK." Her cousin's mother, her aunt, was still alive.

She continued, "She wasn't noticing him. Then he looked at me and said, 'Would you tell my mom I'm OK?'"

Ramona was very happy to have connected with her cousin. I didn't follow up with her about whether she spoke to her aunt.

Other Extraordinary IADC Cases

Many other IADC cases have been extraordinary for a variety of reasons. Every time a patient engages in an IADC experience, the results may be so remarkable that both the patient and therapist are stunned and, at times, inspired by them.

Glenn's Case: "Tommy said, 'It's important that people know about the spiritual world.'"

This IADC was unusually elaborate and the patient experienced connections in it to a real life event. I had several successful IADCs with Glenn, an African-American patient. As we talked during one session, he told me about an unusual occurrence that had happened while he and a friend were riding in his friend's new truck 20 years before. As they passed through an intersection, Glenn was horrified to see a car speeding through the intersection from the right, headed full force toward him. He braced for the collision that might end his life. The speeding car was so close he could see the face of the woman driving it, but she had the most peaceful looking eyes and face he had ever seen. Time froze at that moment. The truck was then hit and rolled two or three times from the impact of the collision, but remarkably, he and his friend were unhurt.

"But that's only part of what was so strange," he said to me. "As I got out of the truck, I had the most peaceful feeling I think I've ever had. I was almost killed, but everything seemed wonderful. I walked home, about 15 miles, but all the way I felt a warm glow. To this day, I don't know what happened. I know this is crazy, but do you think we could find out what happened and why I felt that way 20 years ago?"

After using EMDR with thousands of cases, I had come to believe that anything could emerge during EMDR. I was curious to see whether we could find out anything as well, so I agreed to do EMDR focusing on the event. We started while he held the image of the woman's eyes that he remembered so clearly. I performed EMDR and he closed his eyes. After a moment, he opened them and spoke slowly, with wonder in his voice, "I could see the eyes again. But they weren't the woman's eyes. They were Tommy's eyes."

"Who is Tommy?" I asked.

He told this story. "When I was eight years old, I broke my arm and was in the hospital for a couple of nights. Tommy was my roommate. He was eight years old too. Tommy was white and I wasn't used to white people. So I was surprised to see how upbeat and positive he was, especially since he was an orphan and never received visitors, and he was dying from leukemia. Tommy really seemed to latch onto me. We got to be very close in just a couple of days. Then one night, I was awakened by the sounds of nurses cleaning Tommy's things off his dresser. Tommy had died." He paused and looked at me intently. "It was Tommy's eyes I saw. Do you think Tommy is my guardian angel?"

"I don't know," I replied. "Would you like to ask him?"

"Sure," Glenn responded enthusiastically and shifted into a comfortable position.

We did an IADC induction and Glenn closed his eyes. "I can see Tommy," he said, and sat quietly. IADC sessions normally last around five to 20 seconds; he sat motionless and silent for ten minutes.

Finally, Glenn opened his eyes with a warm smile. "Tommy said, 'Yes, I do watch over you. But sometimes, because of your frame of mind, I can't get through to you.'" Glenn laughed, then continued. "Tommy and I talked and talked. I asked him a lot of questions and he answered every one. One thing Tommy told me was that the aura is the spirit and that time is the key to understanding the spirit world."

Glenn continued telling me what Tommy had said. He was moved and warmed by the experience with this little friend he had forgotten about. When he was finished, I asked Glenn to ask Tommy a question for me. "Glenn, ask Tommy, 'Is inducing IADCs a good thing?'"

I went through the induction procedure with him and he closed his eyes. After a moment, he opened them with a smile on his face. "Yes," he said, "Tommy told me it is a good thing. He said, 'It's important that people know about the spiritual world.' But he said to me, 'Don't fool yourself, though. The deceased are always in control. Don't try to abuse it.'"

Barry's Case: "Why are you still thinking this way? It's not your fault."

Barry's case is another in which the patient had a question answered during an IADC experience.

Ever since his discharge from the army 28 years before his IADC session with me, Barry had been haunted by the loss of two friends in Vietnam. He told me this story as he sat in my office.

During the war, Barry had developed a friendship with a 14-year-old Vietnamese boy. One day, Barry's unit was transporting ammunition by barge on a river and Barry asked the Vietnamese boy to make the trip with them. Barry's best friend in the unit was making the journey as well. One night when his friend was on guard duty, Barry went to his friend's post but couldn't find him. He was going to ask the boy to help him find his friend, but the boy had also mysteriously disappeared.

Three days later, they found his friend's body floating in the river with his throat cut. No one ever saw the Vietnamese boy again. Some in the platoon assumed the boy had been killed too. Barry felt intense loss over the deaths of his two friends.

Barry had already experienced IADCs focusing on other losses and was eager to have an induction to resolve his grief and guilt. I went through the induction process and he closed his eyes, focusing on the soldier who was his friend.

Barry reported that his friend appeared as soon as he closed his eyes and spoke to him: "Why are you still thinking this way? It's not your fault and it doesn't matter how it happened. We were all kids back then. You need to give this up and take better care of yourself. You can see I'm still living; my body is just gone." Barry's sadness and guilt for his friend completely resolved at that moment.

We then attempted an IADC focusing on the Vietnamese boy, but nothing happened. We tried the process again three times, but were unsuccessful. I have no explanation for the lack of success when he had just had a successful IADC. There didn't appear to be anything blocking the experience. That was very odd because Barry had had other successful IADC experiences quickly and easily before and 100 percent of the patients who have successful IADCs have them on successive attempts.

As we discussed why this induction wasn't working, Barry suggested, "Perhaps he's still alive. I bet he was a VC. He killed my friend and then swam ashore. Actually, I feel sure now that's what happened."

While these extraordinary cases are unusual because of their poignancy, drama, or sensory content, some other cases have been even more remarkable. I devote the entire next chapter to them. They are the IADCs that defy what we, who have devoted our lives to the study of psychology, have assumed to be true.

7

IADCs That Defy Known Psychological Theories

Reality is that which, when you stop believing in it, doesn't go away.

—Philip K. Dick, *Do Androids Dream of Electric Sheep?*

As the other psychotherapists on the unit and I spoke about the IADCs and I heard reactions from people outside of the unit who learned about what our patients were experiencing, I began to realize that the issue of whether these events were perceived as real communication with dead people might limit its acceptance by the psychological community and by administrators wary of unusual methods being used in their facilities. I felt then, as I do now, that we need to put aside the issue of whether the IADC phenomenon is communication with the spirit of a dead person. That is simply going to interfere with studying the IADC experience, understanding its remarkable healing properties, and having it be used freely in therapists' offices.

While I realize that people will undoubtedly discuss that issue, and professionals using IADC therapy will surely line up on either side of the fence, I feel the metaphysical speculations should not create prejudices either against IADC therapy or for it. It works, dramatically, so it is worthy of study and common application in therapy. It should not be shunned because it inspires metaphysical speculation.

In a phone call about another matter, I ventured to tell a psychologist not involved with the unit about what I had discovered. His reaction was, "Isn't it remarkable the strange hallucinations the mind can create?" That gave me pause after I hung up the phone. What if these are hallucinations?

The answer came to me almost immediately. If the IADC phenomenon is hallucination, it is a grander hallucination than any ever recorded in the annals of psychology.

It occurred to me that the brain may possess a hidden capability that could be termed the "healing savant" faculty. The inner representation of the deceased described in the grief therapy literature could be the origin of this faculty. It is present in all humans, but this healing savant inner representation capability remains dormant throughout the person's life, appearing unbidden in spontaneous ADCs or when induced by a psychotherapist. This remarkable capability bypasses all of the patient's feelings of anger, guilt, sadness, and traumatic intrusions, rendering them impotent, with no external intervention from the therapist other than the introductory induction procedure.

It convinces the patient, counter to the person's embedded, intransigent, negative emotions, that a deceased person feels differently than the patient believed, and the direction of that different feeling is always positive, in spite of the fact that the patient's traumatic images have all been intensely negative, at times for decades. The healing savant faculty supersedes the person's normal perceptual framework, diagnoses the person's needs, views life and the traumatic events from another perspective, reorients perceptions without influence from the therapist or the person's own consciousness, and sends the mind on its way, blissfully, miraculously, and irreversibly healed.

After completing its work, it retreats, usually without being activated again unless the patient has another induction. The patient, changed irrevocably, returns to a normal daily routine.

I concluded by thinking, if it is a hallucination, then this hallucination is great news!

But what about accompanying pathologies? Does the patient end up with negative side effects if this is a hallucination? The answer came as quickly as the first: It has no residual negative side effects. Patients aren't prone to other hallucinations; they don't lose touch with reality; and they aren't more likely to be hospitalized for pathologies associated with hallucinations. In fact, quite the opposite happens. They leave therapy healed and at times joyful. And in all cases, so far, the positive outcomes persist over time.

IADCs Defy the Experiencer's Perceptual Framework

Perception is our way of interpreting and giving meaning to our ongoing sensory experiences. All perceptions are shaped by five general factors: beliefs, expectations, past experiences, current emotions, and social influence. The more ambiguous the sensory information the perceiver attends to, the more these factors come into play. For example, the perception of a stimulus as vague as an inkblot has much more to do with these internal determinants of perception than they do with the inkblot itself. That is why some psychologists like to give their clients the inkblot test—to uncover a patient's tendency to interpret the world in a particular way.

The IADC cases in this chapter generally violate a person's beliefs, expectations, past experiences, and current emotions. In fact, the IADC procedure requires that these perceptual influences be put on hold for a brief period for the IADC to occur. With regard to social influence, while it may be that the therapist suggests to the client that an IADC experience may be forthcoming, any specific suggestions beyond that will prevent the experience from unfolding. Since vagueness is a prerequisite for a successful IADC induction, it is remarkable that IADC experiences are so consistent in content from person to person.

Wishful thinking on the part of the client also does not seem to account for the content of IADCs. Sometimes, the IADC content is in direct opposition to what the client wishes the IADC experience to be. In a majority of cases, the IADC content includes components that may be welcome, but which were not all wished for or anticipated.

IADCs, in nearly all cases, come as a surprise and are experienced as inconsistent with one's beliefs, expectations, past experiences, current emotions, and wishes. The cases in this chapter illustrate these principles. Any psychological theory used to explain IADCs will have some difficulty because the usual psychological factors do not seem to account for the experiences and are purposefully minimized in the IADC procedure.

The Need for a New Classification for ADCs and IADCs

Nearly all of the many thousands of recorded ADC and IADC experiences have been reported by normal, healthy people who show no signs of pathology associated with hallucinations. If the IADCs are hallucinations, they are different from any other hallucination we know about, and would at least require a distinct classification of human experience.

Hallucinations are perceptions without corresponding sensory input, meaning that a hallucination is all in the subject's head; it is purely subjective. Any explanation for the phenomenon, whether it is judged to be hallucination or not, must account for the occurrences in the IADC cases presented in the previous chapters and those that follow describing patients knowing or experiencing things they likely would not know or simply could not know.

The need for researchers in the field of psychology to study such unusual mental experiences was stated in a book published by the American Psychological Association (APA): *Varieties of Anomalous Experience: Examining the Scientific Evidence* (Cardenia, Lynn, and Krippner 2000). The book's contributors, a number of well-known international authorities in the field of psychology, point out that traditional psychology has long ignored the study of experiences that deviate from the ordinary and challenge standard beliefs about reality. They also make a strong case for the serious study of anomalous experiences so that they can be integrated with psychological research, theory, and practice. I believe that the presentation of the material in this book is consistent with these goals.

Other IADC Observations That Hallucination Theories Will Have to Explain

Hallucination theories must explain other phenomena common among the IADCs we have witnessed:

1. IADCs are remarkably consistent across experiencers, not idiosyncratic as hallucinations are. For example, all deceased appear remorseful or willing to forgive; all have "I'm OK" messages; all contain expressions of unconditional love; none contain fearful characteristics; all exhibit feelings of calm, contentment, and happiness. The list continues. If the phenomena were hallucinations, we would expect a wide variation in tone and content, most of which would reflect the patient's psychological state. That is not the case with IADCs.

2. Many IADCs contain information unknown to the experiencer that is later verified to be true.

3. Experiencers commonly perceive messages they don't want to hear or don't expect to hear and would not be able to imagine because of their psychological limitations.

4. Many messages contain perspectives far beyond the patient's ability to stand outside of the situation, evaluate it, diagnose the need, fabricate the perfect scenario to satisfy the need, enact it in a mental drama, and be so convincing to the psyche that it reverses the patient's beliefs and heals long-standing, intractable trauma and grief. Years of psychotherapy were not able to affect the patient's beliefs that created intense feelings of guilt and anger, but these experiences heal in minutes. The IADC messages violate the patient's belief system by showing it to be misleading or false and the patient accepts the intruding perspective as truth, immediately reversing a deeply rooted belief system without question.

5. Nearly all of the most reliable witnesses, the experiencers themselves, assert strongly, at times defiantly, that they communicated with the deceased. The experiencers assert that they have had no other experiences in their lifetimes that parallel the IADC, unless they have had an NDE or spontaneous ADC experience.

6. The experiences are always positive and loving. They always contain the exact comforting and insightful message the patients need. The experiences are strikingly different from the scenes the patient might construct

from whole cloth, considering the normal inclinations of human beings to be negative, judgmental, and unloving, and the anger and guilt in which the patients are embroiled that brought them to therapy.

7. We now have on record a number of sessions during which people in the room with the experiencer (observers and therapists) have had private mental experiences while the experiencer was quietly having an IADC, and the experiences have been identical to the experiencer's IADCs. Chapter 8 explains these "shared IADCs."

Cases That Illustrate These Observations

The cases that follow illustrate the points that any theory about the origin of IADC healing will have to explain.

Julia Mossbridge's Case: "I see Josh walking toward me, laughing and playing with an angel dog. For now, this is the only kind of proof I need."

After I had spoken a number of times on national and international radio shows, describing the IADC phenomenon, people began asking me for interviews. One was Julia Mossbridge, a reporter for *Conscious Choice* magazine, mother, cognitive neuroscientist, and author.

I induced an IADC for her in which she perceived her reconnection with a friend named Josh who had been killed in an automobile accident. During the IADC, she learned something she did not know before the IADC, and she later verified that it was true. Following is her article about the experience, entitled "Grief Relief: Visiting the Dead" (*Conscious Choice*, November 2003). She mentions the pointer with a blue tip that I have the patient watch instead of my fingers during eye movements.

A friend of mine died when I was in college, and I blamed myself. Josh was not sure he wanted to come to the dance I was deejaying with his sister, but when I flirted a bit during a phone call he decided to make the drive. He never arrived at the dance— he was killed by a truck on the freeway. I had mentally tucked away this episode until I heard of a new technique that uses communication with the deceased as a way to heal unresolved grief.

I was pretty sure I didn't have any residual grief about Josh's death. If anything, I felt only guilt about the role I played in it. Nonetheless, I wondered if I could ask Josh's forgiveness for my role in his death. So I called up the doctor who developed this technique, Allan Botkin, who does his work in Lincolnshire, Illinois.

When I walked into Dr. Botkin's office, I was a little taken aback. I guess I had imagined some sort of high-tech machine in a darkened room presided over by a lab-coat clad, bearded, and eccentric character. Instead, the first thing I saw was a two-foot-long white stick with a blue marker cap on it. Now really, I thought—is this it? A magic wand for seeing dead people? And Dr. Botkin himself, far from a mad scientist type, looked like he belonged at a softball game, giving tips to kids in an avuncular, arm-around-the-shoulder sort of way.

Despite my misgivings, I sat down and listened to his description of "Induced After-Death Communication," which he developed by modifying a biofeedback technique in which the eyes quickly go back and forth. The theory behind this approach is based on the observation that during rapid-eye-movement (REM) sleep, the brain is able to make associations and process information more quickly than during normal waking hours. Imitating REMs in the waking hours is believed to activate the same sort of speedy processing and associative leaps that were previously only attainable during dream states.

Drawing on the decades he spent at the Veteran's Administration treating soldiers with severe grief and trauma, Dr. Botkin explained that each client must be moved from the more superficial emotions—anger, guilt, and shame—into the core sadness that he believes is the root cause of the other emotions. He claimed that using his modified technique (www.induced adc.com) people can safely move through their sadness and release it. Further, about 70 percent of his clients experience after-death communication (ADC)—reconnecting with the bereaved person in a realistic, joyful, inner vision.

As he described the methodology for me in his frank, no-frills way, every one of my intellectual bells went off to tell me that he was pulling my leg. At the same time, I had a strong gut feeling that said he was on to something. Being a good scientist, I trusted my gut. I let him do a short session with me, even though I told him I had no grief.

One minute later, after simply looking at the moving wand and listening to him gently ask me to get in touch with my grief, I was filled with images of my last fateful interaction with Josh. I watched some more waves of the magic wand and started to cry, seeing images of his death. As my sadness began to wane, I got in touch with a happy memory of Josh. Then I closed my eyes and actually had an ADC.

Simply, without pretense, I saw Josh walk out from behind a door. My friend jumped around with his youthful enthusiasm, beaming at me. I felt great joy at the connection, but I couldn't tell whether I was making the whole thing up. He told me I wasn't to blame and I believed him. Then I saw Josh playing with his sister's dog. I didn't know she had one. We said good-bye and I opened my eyes, laughing.

The experience seemed too simple, too light. There were no trumpets, no bright tunnels, just a conversation with Josh. Dr. Botkin had mentioned that people are surprised by how "normal" ADC seems; I certainly was. He also mentioned that neither the therapist nor the client has to believe in the validity of ADC for it to heal—grief is resolved through the reconnection, whether real or imagined.

Later I found out that Josh's sister's dog had died, and it was the same breed as the one I had seen in my vision. Yet I still don't know what's real. What I do know is that when I think of Josh, I no longer dwell on the images of me calling him or of his car getting hit. Instead, I see Josh walking toward me, laughing and playing with an angel dog. For now, this is the only kind of proof I need.

Clay's Case: "Forgive me for being so cold when we adopted you."

What follows is another example of these common cases in which the patient doesn't understand something in the IADC, but learns later the information is true.

Clay's friend Ron had died 23 years before he came to see me. Both were in their twenties at the time. Clay was not in distress about it, but did want to feel a reconnection with his friend. I induced an IADC and Clay reported what happened.

"I can see Ron. He's smiling and saying 'I'm OK.'" Clay stopped for a few seconds with his eyes still closed.

"Why is Andy there?" he asked.

He opened his eyes and explained what had happened. "I saw my friend Ron, and everything was OK. Standing to the back and a little behind him was someone else. It looked like Andy, a friend of mine I used to work with. But his face looked longer and thinner than I remember it."

I suggested that he go back to the scene and clear up the mystery. He agreed and I did another induction. He closed his eyes. After a minute, he opened them.

"That wasn't Andy," he said with his eyes wide. "That was my father, my adoptive father. He always looked like Andy when he was alive, but the guy I just saw looked years younger. That's why his face looked longer and thinner."

He continued, "My father said to me, 'Forgive me for being so cold when we adopted you.' That doesn't make any sense to me. I can't ever remember him being cold to me. He was a wonderful father." Clay then said he forgave his father in the IADC, but didn't really understand what was going on because his father was not cold to him.

That night, Clay called his mother and asked her, "Was Dad cold to me when I was young?"

His mother gasped and said, "Yes. How could you have remembered that? You were only a tiny baby."

Clay didn't elaborate, but said he remembered something and was just curious.

His mother continued, "When you were a baby, your Dad had some difficulty accepting you and wouldn't hold you. But after a few months, everything was fine. How could you remember that?"

Clay went on to tell me that all he could remember of his adoptive father was the love he felt from him and the fun they had fishing and camping together. He had no memory of his father not holding him as an infant, which he perceived his father had been referring to in the IADC.

Jeremy's Case: "The guy saw right through me."

Often patients experience a message directly counter to what they wanted or expected to hear. At times, that message has insights the individuals could not have originated from their conscious intent and psychological position.

While in Vietnam, Jeremy, a blue-eyed Swede from Wisconsin, played football with the black soldiers in his base camp. There was some racial tension and separateness. One day after playing football with these soldiers, Jeremy stayed on the field practicing punts while the others went into the barracks. A sudden attack sent a rocket into the barracks. Jeremy rushed in to find several wounded comrades, including one of the guys he had just been playing football with. Although he hadn't been really friendly with the soldier, he held him and cradled his head as he died in Jeremy's arms.

Jeremy asked to have a session with me because he had "something on his mind." He explained to me that even though he didn't know the black soldier well, he was having intrusive images about the death, so he asked me to use IADC therapy to help him.

After the induction procedure, Jeremy closed his eyes. "I see him, I can see him. He's smiling." He paused and smiled with his eyes still closed. "He just said to me, 'For a white guy, you were all right.'" After a few seconds, he opened his eyes with a questioning look on his face. "You know, I never could remember this guy's name. If I only had his name, I would feel better. Can I do it again and ask him?"

It was obviously important to him, so I agreed and induced another IADC. After a minute, he opened his eyes and shifted uncomfortably in his chair with a frown on his face.

"What happened?" I asked.

He shook his head looking down at the floor. "The guy saw right through me."

"What do you mean?" I asked.

He looked at me and explained, "I asked him his name and he said, 'Why do you want my name now? You didn't want it back then.'" Jeremy looked at me seriously. "Doc, I have a confession to make. I wanted his name so I could put it on the paperwork for my service rating to get more money."

If a veteran can prove a current problem is related to an incident during military service, the vet receives compensation for the trauma in a monthly check. Jeremy needed the black soldier's name because he wanted to fill out new paperwork saying that he was close to him and was now feeling grief over his death. He thought he could get it in an IADC.

"The guy saw right through me," he said again, shaking his head. I provided him with some additional EMDR to reduce his discomfort. He was then able to accept what had happened as a helpful learning experience.

Jeremy and I began to work on other issues and he never brought up the subject again. He had perceived a response to his question about the deceased's name that he did not expect and did not want. Clearly, he was not in conscious control of the contents of the IADC.

Brian's Case: "I feel like I've forgiven him for the first time in 31 years."

When Brian was a medic in Vietnam, he had a difficult relationship with his commanding officer. At one point, someone had stolen Brian's rifle and his officer, not believing his story, ordered Brian to go out on the next mission unarmed, even though other weapons were available. Brian survived the mission, but felt rage toward the officer for putting his life in jeopardy. For 31 years, Brian's anger was as strong every day as it was on the day the incident happened; he believed that if ever saw the officer again, he would kill him.

We talked about the incident and I suggested we do core-focused EMDR therapy on his fear to help him resolve the anger. Along with sadness, fear is another core emotion. We couldn't do an IADC procedure focusing on the commanding officer because Brian was sure he was still alive.

After the feeling of anger and fear had reduced, I gave him one additional set of EMDR movements to help him further relax. He then closed his eyes and immediately saw the commanding officer standing in front of him with a concerned and caring look on his face. Brian reported that the commanding officer said he was very sorry for what he had done and for all the problems that Brian's ongoing anger had caused him in his life.

"He looked like he really meant it," Brian said afterward. "I believe him."

I was amazed because it was the first time a patient had experienced a normal IADC communication with someone who was alive (later came the other two exceptions explained in chapter 6). Despite this departure from the usual, my attitude then and now is that the therapy works. It seemed that we might be introducing a new category: induced communication with living people that heals intrusive memories.

With that, Brian's anger completely resolved. "I feel like I've forgiven him for the first time in 31 years."

After leaving my office, Brian, out of curiosity, went to the book that lists the names of everyone who died in Vietnam. He discovered his officer's name in the book; he was killed soon after Brian left Vietnam.

Juan's Case: "Use your tools."

"Use your tools," Juan said, repeating to me what his father had told him during an IADC induction. Juan's father had always given him good advice when he was alive. Since his father had passed away several months earlier, Juan's grief was heightened by the feeling that he had lost his mentor and advisor as well as beloved father. Before the induction, he told me he was going to ask his father for any advice that might help him in his life now.

The induction started easily. When he opened his eyes after his IADC experience, he said, "I asked him if he had any advice for me. Dad told me, 'Use your tools, Juan.' I can't understand that at all. I have some old tools in the back of the garage, but I haven't used them for years. I don't understand."

"Why don't you go back and ask him what he means," I suggested. I performed another induction and Juan closed his eyes. After a moment, he smiled and nodded his head. He opened his eyes. "I asked him about the tools. He said to me, 'No, Juan, not the ones in your garage. Use the tools you're learning in therapy right now. They are going to make a difference in your life.'"

Juan got a message he did not expect or understand. He had to ask his father for an interpretation of the statement, and the interpretation he arrived at was not one he would have originated from his expectations of what his father might say.

Simon's Case: "I was really hoping to have a message for Darlene."

Another remarkable characteristic of some IADCs must be considered as we look for the sources of this remarkable phenomenon. At times, the patient perceives some message he doesn't understand, and the explanation for the message doesn't come from information the patient has. Only after consulting someone else does the message make sense.

Simon was deeply affected by his good friend Jim's death a month before he came to see me. He had been close to Jim and his wife, Darlene, and was suffering deep grief over his friend's death.

Simon agreed to participate in an IADC to resolve his grief. I did the standard IADC induction and he closed his eyes. In a moment, he smiled. "I can see Jim. He's smiling and waving. I can hear him calling to me." He opened his eyes. "The image was really clear. That makes me feel great. I feel like he's OK. But you know, I was really hoping to have a message for Darlene. She's not doing well at all."

I suggested that he ask Jim for a message. We went through the induction process and he closed his eyes. After a moment, he opened his eyes and looked at me, puzzled. "I didn't see Jim this time. I just saw one hand holding another hand. I could tell the top hand was Jim's because it was broad and veiny, like Jim's were. The other hand seemed to be Darlene's in my understanding. Now that doesn't mean anything to me. It's not much of a message for her."

We ended the session with Simon feeling comforted and happy that he had a sense of reconnection with Jim, although he still didn't understand why he saw Jim's hand on Darlene's when he asked for a message for her.

Later that day, Simon called me excitedly. "Well, Dr. Al," he said, "I went to Darlene's right away and told her about seeing Jim. She was really happy. I told her that I did ask him for a message for her, but he didn't give me one. I just saw a very clear image of his hand holding hers. She began to cry, smiling and nodding her head. She told me, 'Last night I had a dream. It was so clear it didn't seem like a dream. I felt, really felt, Jim holding my hand. Simon, he did give you a message from him to me. He was saying that it really was him holding my hand last night.'"

Simon's grief remained resolved from that time through my last contact with him.

Vera's Case: "Can I do it again? I want to hear her say it again."

Patients' perceptions of the deceased often take a humorous turn when the deceased upbraids the patient in a familiar manner, something the patient would not expect to experience in the IADC. Vera's IADC is an example.

Vera's mother had died suddenly in the night three months before she came to me for grief therapy, so Vera was still in the grieving process. She agreed to experience an IADC to help her with her sadness.

I did three inductions, and on the third Vera almost immediately experienced her mother telling her she should be happy because her mother was happy. Vera was elated. She enjoyed the experience so much she wanted to return to the IADC to ask her mother a question. I administered a set of eye movements and told her to close her eyes and keep thinking about her mother. After a few seconds, she opened her eyes, beaming. "She answered me," she said, delighted. "I want to ask her again. Can I do that?"

"Sure," I responded. I administered a set of eye movements and she closed her eyes again. She opened her eyes after a few seconds, bubbling with excitement. "I asked her and she told me the same thing. Can I do it again? I want to hear her say it again."

It was obvious that Vera was having the same euphoria I had seen in many other patients who experienced IADCs. While she couldn't think of anything else to ask, she wanted to keep having the experience. I induced an IADC again.

After a few seconds, Vera opened her eyes wide, drawing back the corners of her mouth and lowering her head in an "oops" look.

"What happened?" I asked with great curiosity.

"Mom said to me, 'Why do you keep asking me the same question? I already gave you the answer.' I guess I overdid it."

Shared IADCs: An Even Stronger Argument against a Hallucination Explanation for the IADC Phenomenon

The cases presented in this chapter appear to defy current psychological theories. The explanation eventually formulated for the source of IADCs will have to address these issues. Though they are remarkable, the content of these cases is not the strongest argument that current psychological theories are inadequate to explain IADCs. In the next chapter, we present the phenomenon of *shared* IADCs—two people having the same private experience at the same time.

8

Shared IADCs and Concurrent ADCs

A human being is part of the whole, called by us "Universe"; a part limited in time and space. He experiences himself, his thoughts and feelings as something separated from the rest—a kind of optical delusion of his consciousness. This delusion is a kind of prison for us, restricting us to our personal desires and to affection for a few persons nearest us. Our task must be to free ourselves from this prison by widening our circle of compassion to embrace all living creatures and the whole of nature in its beauty. Nobody is able to achieve this completely but the striving for such achievement is, in itself, a part of the liberation and a foundation for inner security.

—Albert Einstein (quoted in H. Eves, *Mathematical Circles Adieu*)

Probably the most unusual occurrences we have experienced happened at first by accident with professionals not susceptible to confusing illusion with reality. We were then able to induce the occurrence intentionally with other therapists and patients in several trials. We have not been able to understand it yet, but the phenomenon should be studied and must be taken into account as we determine the classification for ADCs, NDEs, and IADCs.

We discovered that an observer in the room with the patient and psychotherapist as the IADC occurs seems to be able to eavesdrop on the internal IADC experience the patient is having. The preliminary evidence for the eavesdropping appears strong, and it was replicated across therapists, observers, and patients. We came to call the incidents "shared IADCs." A variant of it, in which the observer experienced a separate ADC during the same session and involving the same deceased people that appeared in the patient's IADC, we termed "concurrent ADCs."

Shared IADCs

The first time I became aware of the shared IADC phenomenon, I was inducing an IADC while a psychologist I was training observed. The patient wanted to resolve his grief by having an IADC of his deceased uncle, with whom he had spent much of his youth. While I induced the IADC with the patient, the observing psychologist closed his eyes and performed the eye movements himself to relax.

Images appeared to the psychologist in training: a vivid scene of a swampy area with cattails, a pond, and a willow tree. He felt as though he was lying on the grass with the pond at eye level. It made no sense to him, so he opened his eyes and continued to observe the patient and me. The patient had not yet begun speaking, so the psychologist had no knowledge of what the patient was experiencing during the IADC.

When the patient opened his eyes after the IADC, he said he saw a swamp scene. He felt like he was lying in the grass looking at the swamp. The psychologist in training was surprised at this coincidence and asked, "Did you see cattails?"

The patient said, "Yes," not expecting that to be an unusual statement since he had said it was a swamp.

The psychologist then said, "Did you see a pond and a willow tree?"

The patient was clearly surprised. "Yes," he said. "How did you know that?"

The psychologist explained what he had done and the two continued to compare notes with great accuracy between their reports of what they had experienced.

One part of the scene did not match, however. The psychologist asked, "Did you see the ducks fly overhead?"

The patient said, "No, that's the one thing you've described that I didn't see."

I asked the patient, "Why did you see a swamp?"

The patient answered, "The swamp was in the backyard of my uncle's farm. I used to play there and would lie in the grass by the pond."

The patient, psychologist, and I sat with wide eyes. Then they looked to me for insights, as though my training in psychology had covered what to say in a situation like this. They didn't know it, but I was as shocked as they were. I maintained my professional demeanor, but admitted that I didn't know what had happened. After the session ended, I walked out the back door of the building and through the hospital grounds alone, lost in thought about this unexplainable occurrence.

In the next session with this patient and the same psychologist observer, the patient said he was eager to learn more about this occurrence and agreed to do it again, so I induced an IADC with the patient while the psychologist self-induced an IADC. The two sat quietly for a while. Finally, they opened their eyes and, before the patient explained his IADC, the psychologist reported that he had perceived a conversation between the patient and his uncle. He provided specific details about it while the patient and I listened. Afterward, the patient responded that all the details matched the conversation he had experienced in his IADC.

We were intrigued by this development, so the observer psychologist and I experimented with eight other patients who agreed to participate. This time, the psychologist wrote down everything he experienced before the patients reported what happened during their IADCs. In every instance, the psychologist's accounts matched the patients' IADCs with great accuracy.

Another Psychologist Shares an IADC with Her Patient

I explained this finding to another psychologist whom I had trained in IADC therapy. She reported the next day that, during a session, she had given herself eye movements while her patient experienced an IADC, and she had an IADC-type experience. This is what she reported to me:

After you described to me what had happened with the shared IADC, I was curious about whether any person present during the patient's IADC experience might share the IADC, including the psychotherapist. So I decided to give it a try. I was working with a patient who had both traumatic images and grief from a war experience. He was hoping to IADC one of the soldiers he had seen die during a fierce battle.

After the usual induction, I knew he was ready for the IADC because I had brought him to a receptive state. I administered a set of eye movements and he closed his eyes. At the same time, I closed my eyes and moved them. What I experienced was incredible. I wasn't trying to experience anything, but very vivid scenes of a soldier in a peaceful, green valley started coming to me. I could sense that he was communicating and saying, "It's all right. It wasn't your fault."

I opened my eyes after a short time to be sure I was watching my patient when he opened his. Soon after he opened his eyes, he told me, "I saw him. It was really him. He said not to keep feeling bad. It wasn't my fault." Well, I was pretty stunned, but I stayed with it.

"Describe what you saw," I said, curious to see what he would describe. "What was the scenery like?"

He said to me, and these were his words: "It was a beautiful lush, green place with slight rises on either side like a valley." I kept my composure and we finished the session. I wasn't willing to tell him what had just happened, and now that I know what can happen, I won't do it again without talking to the patient about it first. But someone really has to study this.

I caution that we would not condone participating in such an experience without the patient's permission and foreknowledge about what was occurring. I personally have not engaged in sharing an IADC with a patient because of my concerns about privacy.

One of the Trained Psychotherapists
Experiences a Shared IADC during a Session

Dr. David Mannelli, whom I had trained a few years earlier, became very successful at inducing IADCs in his practice in Milwaukee, Wisconsin.

He e-mailed me one day to explain the remarkable shared IADC he had experienced. This is his account of what happened:

> I was counseling a 40-year-old mother of two who had lost her husband about a year before our session. I did the standard core-focused EMDR, but her grief wouldn't diminish the way it normally does when we prepare for the IADC induction, so we went through four sessions of EMDR focusing on her grief. During that time, I developed a strong rapport with her and felt a real understanding of her grief and empathy with her. Finally, during the fifth session, she seemed to be ready and I used EMDR to relax her into a receptive state. The IADC unfolded.
>
> During the quiet time when she was experiencing her IADC with her eyes closed, I closed my eyes for a few seconds and did eye movements myself. I experienced a clear image of a man in a bright white shirt, young and healthy, holding his hand over his heart.
>
> After she opened her eyes, she explained to me, full of joy, that she had experienced a visual image of her husband and the "essence" of what he was feeling. I asked her what he looked like. She replied, "He had on a very bright white shirt, and he looked younger and completely healthy. He was holding his hand over his heart."

Six months after telling me about this session, Dave reported to me that the patient had called to thank him and said her family and friends had noticed a glow about her since the therapy session.

Generalizations about Shared IADCs

The shared IADC experience was a turning point for me in my understanding of the IADC phenomenon. After witnessing a number of shared IADCs myself, I realized that it was unlikely that IADCs could be hallucinations. A hallucination is idiosyncratic—two people cannot have identical hallucinations at the same time. During shared IADCs, the experiencers are observing the same reality, so it probably is independent of both of them. Further study of the phenomenon is warranted.

In all cases of shared IADCs we have recorded, the observers had experienced their own IADC before the shared IADC episode. That seems to sensitize them to the IADC experience. The observers also had a rapport with the IADC experiencer from listening to the experiencer's story and understanding the accompanying grief.

I and my colleagues did attempt to replicate shared IADCs under controlled conditions. In our informal experiment, we used two observers who had had several successful shared IADCs. As a control, the observer had no knowledge of the patient's issues because we had the observer come into the session just before the induction, completely uninformed about the patient's case. When we tried it this way, the shared IADC did not occur.

Dr. Mannelli, the psychotherapist from Milwaukee who experienced one of the shared IADCs, finished his account with these words, which may be the profound insight into shared IADCs: "I firmly believe that the energy of an IADC is linked to the power of love. The stronger the empathy of the therapist, the greater the likelihood of tapping into an IADC."

Concurrent ADCs during an IADC Session

After I had done several interviews with publications, radio, and television describing IADC therapy, psychotherapists from around the nation began to contact me for training. One of these was Hania Stromberg, who has a psychotherapy practice in Albuquerque, New Mexico. She came to Illinois for training and, after she returned to New Mexico, began using IADC therapy as one of the tools to help her patients with their intrusive images and grief.

Hania Stromberg: A Spontaneous ADC before Her Client's IADC

Several weeks after her training, Hania called me excitedly. "Al, this is unbelievable," she said. "I had the experience of hearing my patient's father while he was having an IADC." This is the account of what happened in her words:

> Arnold came to me because he was feeling grief over his father's death. His mother had died years earlier and he and his father lived together until his father's death. His father was a star athlete who excelled at sports in high school and college. It

seemed that he was successful at every sport he tried. In spite of his success in sports and later in business, he said his father felt disappointed in life.

Arnold was very sad about his relationship with his father because he felt his father had not really wanted him. His father developed Alzheimer's disease near the end of his life and Arnold had him placed in a nursing home. That caused him to feel tremendous guilt from a sense that he was simply adding to his father's disappointment with life. He acknowledged that his father was not conscious of where he was during that time, but he still felt guilt for not being able to keep his father at home.

I went through the induction process while Arnold focused on his father. During the EMDR eye movements, I felt what seemed to me like someone entering the room and I said, "Oh, a strong presence just entered the room." Arnold replied immediately, "Yes, yes. I felt the same thing. My father is here."

He closed his eyes. In my mind, I heard a male voice saying, "My son, my dear, dear son," but I didn't share that with the patient. At that, I closed my eyes for a few seconds and saw moving purple swirls.

After a minute, he opened his eyes and described his experience. He said he felt like he was floating and seeing profiles in shadow that looked like his father, floating around him. He then said, "I saw the profiles in swirling waves of purple."

Shortly after that, the session ended.

In the following session, he reported that he had felt blissful for a day after the last session. He had come to feel less guilt and more love for his father. I did the IADC preparation and, after a set of eye movements, Arnold closed his eyes and described what he was seeing. "I see a lot of men in 1950s clothing, very professional and clean cut."

Arnold sat quietly for about ten minutes. Then he opened his eyes with a smile and told me what happened. "I saw Dad and we talked about my life. I asked him whether the woman I'm seeing would be a good match for me. He said 'No, no, my son, my dear, dear son. She's not good for you.'"

I noticed he reported his father saying the exact words I had heard at the previous session, which Arnold had not heard during that session. I asked him, "You said your father said to you, 'My son, my dear, dear son.' Did he say that to you before?"

"Oh, yes," Arnold replied. "He said that to me often when he was alive and I heard him saying it again today."

A Trained Psychologist Has an ADC Experience While Sitting in on His Wife's IADC Session

Sometimes I do the training in how to perform the IADC induction in one-on-one sessions at my office rather than with a group. I spent one Saturday training Don Dufford, Ph.D., a psychologist from San Jose, California. He brought his wife, Ilianna, with him, providing us with a unique opportunity for him to observe me as I performed an IADC induction with her regarding her deceased mother.

We went through the normal induction process and she closed her eyes. She was unusually quiet and I asked, "Are you experiencing anything?" She whispered, "Wait." She sat quietly for another few minutes. I noticed that her husband had his eyes closed while she was having the IADC, and he at one point smiled broadly and laughed to himself.

When she opened her eyes, she explained that she had experienced a very extensive and moving IADC with both her mother and father.

She explained it to me and her husband said that while his eyes were closed, he had the experience of seeing and speaking to his wife's mother and father. "But I didn't have the same experience Ilianna was describing," he explained. "First I connected with them individually. Then, a few minutes later in a separate ADC, I saw Ilianna's mom and dad together dancing and laughing. When I closed my eyes that time I felt such a bright, happy energy emanating from them it really made me smile. It impressed me how distinctly different their energy was from the fatigue I was feeling after a long day of training. It reinforced for me the sense that it was real and that it originated from a source outside of me."

He looked at his wife. "Your mother made me laugh. She called me Dan instead of Don in a kidding way. Remember she used to do that and it became an ongoing joke between us?"

He then took Ilianna's hand and said, "Ilianna, your father said to me very clearly, 'Hi, Don. You know she's my little girl, take care of her.'" Ilianna and Don smiled warmly at each other with tears in their eyes.

The Remarkable Nature of the Shared IADC Phenomenon

Shared IADCs must be studied to understand the nature of this unprecedented phenomenon that defies what we have believed to be true about the brain and consciousness. For me, witnessing them was a turning point in my view of IADCs. To preclude the afterlife explanation, skeptics may have to argue that two people sharing an IADC really aren't sharing a perception of spirits of the deceased, but are somehow magically, telepathically sharing the same hallucination. I was surprised when I sometime later discovered that shared IADCs have a parallel in NDE research. Dr. Moody's discovery of the "shared NDE" is discussed in chapter 13.

9

Professionals and Academics Experience IADCs

By far, the best proof is experience.

—Sir Francis Bacon

Over the years since the discovery of the IADC procedure, I have had the pleasure of describing the IADC phenomenon with many professional mental health providers, physicians, and academics. A number of them were eager to understand IADCs and permitted me to help them experience their own. After the sessions, their certainty that the experience unfolds without conscious leading and that the communications were real paralleled the testimonies of all my patients.

We would assume that the members of these professional groups are balanced and psychologically healthy. The accounts of these trained professionals helped me come to know that IADCs occur in intelligent, educated, psychologically healthy people from all backgrounds and professions.

In the five cases that follow, IADCs were experienced by medical and academic professionals, namely two psychologists, two medical doctors, and a history professor.

Psychologist Joe's Case: "I was surprised by the way my experience unfolded."

Joe is a psychologist. He knew that spontaneous ADC experiences resulted in healing emotional wounds, but was very skeptical about inducing ADCs. He wanted to find out about the practice for himself, so he traveled to my office for an IADC session.

We began by discussing IADCs, and I described an example case. When I asked him to choose the person he wanted to reconnect with, he chose his father. Three years before our session, Joe's elderly father had developed pneumonia after heart surgery and died. "I had an overall positive relationship with my father, but I did have some unfinished business," Joe said. "He was insensitive and critical many times during my life, and that created real problems for me. But what really bothers me now is that he was very afraid of death and never came to terms with his illness."

The first induction attempt was not successful because Joe was trying to imagine a scene similar to the IADC case we discussed at the beginning of the session. I explained that IADCs take a variety of forms, and any attempt on his part to create the experience would prevent an IADC from occurring. I reminded him simply to be open to whatever happened.

We did another induction. Joe sat quietly with his eyes closed, then spoke. "I can see a small bright light. It's getting larger and larger. Now I see a vague image of my father's face, floating out of the light. I can hear him saying, 'Son . . . Son' very warmly and lovingly. I have the feeling he's searching for me and wants to speak with me."

Joe reported that his image then faded, so I provided another induction. "I can see a bright, misty, formless scene, but I can hear my father saying, 'I'm OK. Joe, everything is OK.'" Tears rolled down Joe's face. "These are tears of happiness," he said.

Afterward, Joe said he felt connected to his father in a very loving way, more deeply than he ever had before. He believed that when his father said, "Joe, everything is OK," he meant people shouldn't be tormented by imagined fears about death.

"This is exactly what I needed," Joe continued, "but I didn't realize I needed it. I have a real sense of well-being, a feeling different from any feeling I've had before. I was surprised by the way my experience unfolded. I didn't expect to see the light; that materialized on its own."

I talked with Joe on the phone a few months later. He said he believed all of his issues related to his father's death were resolved. And every time he recalled the IADC experience, he felt the same warm sense of well-being.

Psychologist Cindy's Case: "I think I realize now that much of my strength as a person came from my father's influence."

Cindy was a skeptic before her IADC training, but when she successfully induced IADCs for some of her patients, she was very impressed with the results. She decided to attempt to self-induce an IADC to resolve some issues with her father. Although her father had been dead for almost five years, she continued to have ambivalent feelings toward him. Her father had been a high-ranking military officer who served in WWII, Korea, and the Cuban missile crisis. Unfortunately, his military experiences had made him anxious, unpredictable, and explosive—behavior patterns that led to many family crises and some lingering issues for Cindy.

This is Cindy's account of what happened as she explained it to me. Cindy performed the procedure on herself while sitting quietly at home. She immediately saw her father sitting in a chair in what appeared to be a tropical setting. "He looked younger, thinner, and with more hair, just as he did at an earlier age," she said. "He also appeared happy and peaceful."

Cindy then asked her father what she should do about her sister, who was having problems at the time. He replied, "Nothing. Just relax." She reported that he then looked thoughtful and said, "I hope that at some time you'll be able to find something good in you that you got from me." She said there was a touch of sadness in his voice, but it was more of an empathic sadness than a concern for his own well-being.

Cindy told me that she then opened her eyes, and although she retained a sense of peace from her experience, she also felt perplexed. She did not go back to another IADC at that time.

After she finished telling me the story, I advised her to take her father's statement seriously because it sounded important. She said her disappointment and anger about her relationship with her father made it difficult for her to come up with an immediate response to him. She agreed to allow me to use EMDR to help her process what her father told her in her IADC.

I performed the EMDR process and she closed her eyes. After a moment, she spoke: "I have the sense that despite all of my father's stressors, he remained true blue to Mom and us, even though at times, he appeared down for the count. I think I realize now that much of my strength as a person came from my father's influence."

That night, Cindy self-induced another IADC. When she experienced him again, he looked peaceful and happy, but this time all of his concern for her well-being was gone. Cindy told me later, "It looked like all of his troubles and his concern about the effect they had on me had disappeared." She said her father then told her he was patiently waiting for her mother.

Cindy's issues resolved and the changes were maintained at a one-year follow-up. She believed the experience had further strengthened her so she was able to deal more effectively with an authority figure who reminded her of her father.

In her own experience and in inducing IADCs with her patients, Cindy is certain that the phenomenon is a natural ability that resides in every human being.

Physician Pam's Case: "I have the sense that she is not gone and will always be with me."

Pam is a successful physician who maintains a demanding professional schedule. She came to me because of her feelings of guilt and sadness over her mother's death. She was initially skeptical about the IADC procedure, but agreed to try it.

Pam's mother had died nearly 30 years earlier, when Pam was 14. She and her mother were the only females in the family, so they had developed a very close relationship. Soon after Pam's fourteenth birthday, her mother sat with her on the couch, held her hands, and told her that she had inoperable breast cancer. She said she had only a few months to live. Over the next months, in denial, Pam kept involving her mother in her activities, hoping her mother's active behavior would prove it wasn't true.

Her mother's health deteriorated quickly, however, and three months later, she passed away. After her mother's death, Pam's father and three brothers grieved her death, but Pam believed it was her job to take her mother's place as the strong one in the family, so she never fully addressed her own issues about her mother's death. Her oldest brother blamed Pam for their mother's rapid demise because her mother tried to stay active during her illness by doing things with Pam even though she was exhausted.

Pam maintained a grueling schedule most of her life to avoid feeling her guilt and sorrow. She went through a year and a half of psychotherapy with another therapist and made some progress in allowing herself to express her grief, but the improvements had done little to reduce her feelings of guilt and sadness over her mother's death.

After she finished telling me about her mother, I used core-focused EMDR to go to her sadness and help her start to bring it down. Then I performed the IADC procedure.

After a minute, she opened her eyes and explained what had happened. She said she felt like she was going through a tunnel toward a bright light, but found herself becoming frustrated because she couldn't get to the end of the tunnel. I assured her that the IADC would unfold naturally; she just needed to relax and let it happen.

After some EMDR to relax her and help her move into a receptive state, she was ready for the IADC experience. This time her mother was there. Pam kept her eyes closed for five minutes, a relatively long IADC. Tears rolled down her face as she sat quietly with her eyes closed. Finally, she opened her eyes and said, excitedly, "I saw my mother very clearly. She looked younger and thinner even though she had put on weight the last ten years of her life. She looked healthy, happy, peaceful, and she had a spark in her eyes that seemed to emanate a glow around her."

Pam laughed and said, "My mother was sitting on a large rock by the beach in one of those old-style bathing suits, but the surroundings were more beautiful than any beach scene I've ever seen. She communicated to me in a very clear way that she was very proud of what I had accomplished in my life. She said there was no reason for me to feel guilty about anything. I felt a warm connectedness like we used to have. When Mom was alive, there was always a touch of sadness in her smile, but that was gone and she looked genuinely happy."

When she was finished describing the IADC, she said, "I can't believe how peaceful I feel, like there's been a tremendous burden lifted off of me. And I have the sense that she is not gone and will always be with me."

As she was preparing to leave, she said she felt like all her issues related to the death of her mother had completely resolved. She emphasized more than once how unexpected her experience was.

Two months later she reported that she continued to feel much better, and that she could still experience the warm connectedness with her mother.

History Professor Jane's Case: "She said to me, 'You know you're being ridiculous. Get over it.'"

Jane's mother had been a source of encouragement and inspiration to her—a friend as well as a mother. When Jane completed her doctorate in American history and sought a teaching position, she limited herself to colleges in the Northwest so she could stay close to her mother in Oregon. Their favorite activity for the past three years had been seeing *The Lord of the Rings* movies together.

A year before my session with Jane, her mother had died suddenly from a burst brain aneurysm.

Jane received the news in a California hospital where she was recuperating from delicate surgery. She was heartbroken that she was unable to travel to her mother's funeral. Losing her beloved mother so suddenly and missing the funeral caused her great guilt and sadness. The painful emotions increased over the ensuing year until she came to me, seeking some relief.

Jane told me that she had strong beliefs about the afterlife because of several spontaneous ADCs she had experienced. Her beliefs and ADC experiences were insufficient, however, to help her cope with her mother's death and her feelings of guilt over not attending the funeral. "I should know better," she said to me tearfully, "but I just feel so bad about not seeing her again, even at her funeral."

I took her through the IADC induction process two times without an IADC occurring. On the third try, the IADC unfolded. She sat quietly for a moment, then suddenly laughed. After a minute, she opened her eyes and explained to me what she experienced.

"Mom said to me, 'You know you're being ridiculous. Get over it.' That made me laugh. It was just like her."

She said she felt overwhelming relief and, in fact, was surprised at how relieved she felt. At the next session, she reported to me that she had gone to see a *Lord of the Rings* movie for the first time since her mother's death. Prior to her IADC, even seeing the title *The Lord of the Rings* would reignite her sadness because they so enjoyed seeing the movies together. She said she thoroughly enjoyed the movie and had only happy thoughts about her mother. She felt her mother was with her in some way as she watched the movie.

Cardiac Surgeon Bob's Case: "You really don't expect me to say that was actually my brother, do you?"

This case illustrates how some skeptics remain skeptical even after their successful IADC experience. The important agent in the healing, however, is not what the patient believes, but the experience of reconnection itself.

"This is all a bunch of baloney," Bob announced to me on the phone. Bob was a successful cardiac surgeon who had been referred to me by the leader of a grief group because of his despondence over his brother's long, slow, painful death five years earlier. His grief was so strong that the group was unable to help him.

"Dr. Botkin," he said to me on the phone, "I respect your credentials and the practice of psychotherapy, but I've researched EMDR, ADCs, and IADCs on the Internet and want to cancel the appointment. It's not for me."

"Then I'll give you the session for free," I responded. I knew that if he had a successful IADC, it would relieve him of his grief and open him up to this new therapy. I had seen it work so successfully so many times that I couldn't bear to allow him to walk away from the opportunity to relieve his tormenting grief without trying it.

He agreed reluctantly and the next week was sitting in my office describing his deep sadness over his brother Frank's death. Then he launched into a bitter indictment of his parents for not getting his brother to the hospital sooner when he displayed symptoms of the condition that eventually killed him. As his voice raised, his face contorted into an angry red mask and he sat tensely bolt upright.

I addressed his sadness directly using EMDR and it increased from a 2 to a 9 over three sets of eye movements. I brought his sadness down and then used EMDR to relax him into a receptive state. He closed his eyes.

Bob sat quietly for a couple of minutes, then opened his eyes and slumped in his chair. He looked at me with a weak smile on his face. The tension in his body and face was gone. I asked him how he felt. "I feel tired," he said slowly. He turned his head slightly, looking at me out of the corner of his eye. "You really don't expect me to say that was actually my brother, do you?"

I shrugged my shoulders and said, "It's up to you to believe whatever you want to believe. So what happened?"

"I just had a very weird hallucination," he said. "It seemed that I imagined Frank telling me he loves me, he's OK, and to forgive Mom and Dad. A weird hallucination."

Dr. Bob left a short time later without paying me, as we had agreed, and without a thank you or even a handshake. I never saw him again.

On follow-up, however, his referring counselor reported that when Bob returned to the group he was much more relaxed, even jovial. All of his characteristic grief behavior and talk had vanished, which was very unusual. He quit attending his grief group soon after that, without providing his counselor with an explanation for his disappearance.

I was confident that Dr. Bob got what he needed for his grief, but, as is typical with most IADC experiencers, his character remained intact after the experience. As is the case with all IADCs, the therapeutic effects are limited to the specific grief issue addressed, and do not alter the basic personality structure.

10

Forgiveness in IADCs
Heals Anger and Guilt

Holding on to anger is like grasping a hot coal with the intent of
throwing it at someone else; you are the one who gets burned.

—Buddha

Sometimes a simple IADC reconnection experience and reduction
in sadness from knowing that the deceased is OK are not enough to
resolve intense anger and guilt. In these cases, pointed experiences during the IADC always directly address the anger and guilt. So far, my experience and that of my colleagues who use IADC has been that all issues
that need to be resolved are resolved in the IADC. These issues range
from simple unfinished business ("I didn't say I love you enough") to
forgiveness of someone who has inflicted horrendous acts of cruelty and
violence.

The IADC phenomenon has demonstrated the truth of the aphorism
that forgiveness heals both the forgiver and the forgiven. Many of the healing IADCs we have heard our patients describe contain examples of the
deceased forgiving them or of them forgiving the deceased.

The experience of guilt is a normal, healthy psychological function. Conscience and consideration for others guide our behavior, so when we do something in conflict with our conscience, we experience the unpleasant feeling of guilt. To avoid the aversive guilt feelings, we likely will alter future behavior to appease our conscience. For some, most notably psychopaths or people with antisocial personality disorder (antisocials), conscience and its handmaiden, guilt, play minor roles in shaping behavior. They show no remorse after inflicting pain on others or even murdering them. These people would not be interested in experiencing an IADC since they feel no sadness or guilt. They clearly need to feel more guilt, not less.

Some who read the cases of abuse or cruelty presented in this book may believe that the patients' actions should not be forgiven. They may feel that the deceased's freely given forgiveness and the patients' release from feelings of guilt resulting from a single episode of contrition during the IADC would lead to a license to harm others with impunity and to a kind of widespread moral chaos. That is clearly not the case.

Some of our patients' lives are shredded by guilt from their conviction that they have committed unforgivable acts. When their guilt is resolved in an IADC, even in cases of horrific wrongdoing, the patient's conscience is actually strengthened! Without exception, the experience of reconnection with the deceased results in feelings of love and forgiveness and an increased ability to love and care for others.

The counterpart of the deceased forgiving a patient who inflicted abuse is the experience of the patient forgiving the deceased when the deceased was the perpetrator and the patient was the victim. I must admit that at times I listen to my patients describing the horrors of their childhood or adult trauma with a feeling that the actions of the deceased were unforgivable. How does one forgive a father who sexually and physically abused a little child for years, stunting the child's emotional growth and creating intrusive memories that fill her days with guilt, self-hatred, and relived terror? If I or any other reasonable person feels the deceased is unforgivable, how could the person who experienced the atrocities forgive?

Regardless of the gravity of the traumas the deceased inflicted, however, the patients consistently describe the deceased as being deeply remorseful and apologetic, taking responsibility for their actions and asking for forgiveness. In every case, the patient forgives the deceased and, in every case, the anger dramatically decreases from that moment.

This chapter contains descriptions of IADCs in which patients' experiences of forgiving the deceased or being forgiven by the deceased result in immediate reduction of anger and guilt.

The Person Seeking Forgiveness Must Be Genuinely Remorseful

I have worked with few psychopaths, antisocials, and others with weak or no consciences. I have never attempted an IADC with these patients because they experience no sadness for the deceased. Nearly all of the patients I see who did something terrible to the deceased feel deep remorse, sorrow, or guilt. When the patient feels guilt and sadness about what he or she did to the deceased, it is not from a fear of retribution; it is from a genuine compassion for the victim.

By the same token, all of my patients who have suffered at the hands of the deceased have desired a reconnection to experience a measure of reconciliation. Unless the person has a weak conscience or no conscience, my experience has been that all people have an underlying sense of humanity and compassion that draws them to want to reconnect with the offender or offended to forgive or feel forgiven.

It seems that forgiveness and healing can only occur when the patient feels and fully accepts sadness for the victims or perceives the deceased as being genuinely remorseful. Although I have worked with no patient who did not want to forgive or feel forgiven, I believe that if someone felt no remorse, the forgiving IADC would not occur. That feeling of connection with the humanity of the deceased and resulting compassion must precede the reconnection and forgiveness. Genuine remorse is necessary.

When the patients allow themselves to feel sadness for the victim, they open their own reservoirs of compassion and humanity. Patients often come to the therapy session with mixtures of anger, guilt, and coldness toward others. Through core-focused EMDR, I bypass those feelings and go to the core sadness that is precipitating the defenses. After the forgiving IADC, the sadness, anger, guilt, and coldness disappear, leaving the compassion that is at the base of the patient's being. The patients report that when the deceased has been cruel to them, they perceive the deceased as feeling deep, sorrowful remorse. When they forgive the deceased, their anger, blame, and coldness markedly reduce.

After the experiences of feeling forgiven by the deceased and forgiving the deceased, patients report that their relationships with people around them, especially their families, improve dramatically.

Forgiving heals. That isn't simply an aphorism; it is a clinical observation.

Forgiving the Deceased Heals Anger

Sometimes survivors feel anger toward the deceased because of unresolved conflicts, including abuse. The sense of reconnection and experience of forgiving the deceased result in the healing of their anger. To illustrate, we begin with a mild case and end with a severe one.

Jim's Case: "I both love and forgive my father. I could actually feel him hugging me."

Jim was a very successful businessman who had been in psychotherapy with me for several weeks when he brought up an unresolved issue with his father who had died when Jim was 12. His alcoholic father had been emotionally cold and distant. Jim felt a mixture of sadness and anger about his father's death. "He wasn't there when I needed him," he told me.

Jim agreed to allow me to guide him into an IADC, though he was skeptical. "It sounds a little weird to me."

I took Jim through the IADC procedure and he immediately saw his father. "He looks happier and healthier than when he was alive, and he's younger." Jim reported that he asked his father, "Do you have anything to say for yourself?" referring to his emotional coldness toward Jim.

Jim said that, at that point, he experienced his father moving toward him and embracing him. He said he could feel his father's love for him in a way he never had before. The image of his father then rapidly faded. Jim told me, "I both love and forgive my father. I could actually feel him hugging me."

Jim was very surprised by his experience. When I asked him what he thought about it, he said emphatically, "I'm sure that was really my father; there is no way I could have thought that up in a million years."

Jim then said that he no longer felt any sadness or anger toward his father and that he had only good feelings about him. When I saw Jim two years later, he reported that his issues with his father had remained completely resolved and that all of his thoughts about his father were pleasant. He also said that although he continued to believe that he had actually communicated with his father, he had told only his wife about it because he didn't think anyone would believe him.

Christopher's Case: "Whatever you do, don't commit suicide. Don't give up."

One of the most moving cases I've been involved in was Christopher's. His father had abused him and his sisters severely during Christopher's youth. Christopher had great difficulty describing what had happened because when he brought the memories to the surface, he immediately felt such anxiety that he had to get up and leave.

Finally, he managed to get enough of the story out for me to realize what a hell he and his sisters had lived in during their childhoods. His mother feared her husband and stayed away from the home when she knew he was going to come home drunk. His father would go out drinking and bring home his drunken friends who would physically and sexually abuse Christopher and his two sisters. On one occasion, Christopher was locked in a closet and heard his sisters screaming for hours as the men abused them.

While still a teenager, one of his sisters, Jill, committed suicide. The other, Fran, had killed herself a few weeks before he came to see me. The nightmares and intrusive memories were driving him to continual thoughts of suicide. His anger was so strong that he at times broke furniture in fits of rage.

We agreed to focus on Fran who had killed herself recently. I did sets of eye movements to get in touch with the sadness. I continued to bring him into the sadness through core-focused EMDR until it peaked. More eye movements started to bring it back down. I told him to think of Fran in a general way and went through the IADC induction process three times. On the third set of eye movements, he closed his eyes and the IADC began.

He opened his eyes after a minute, with tears flowing. "I could see my sister in my mind," he said. "She looked very happy though. I've never seen her happy. She said she was sorry about the suicide because she knew what it did to me. Then she said something wonderful." He stopped and shook his head, wiping the tears from his eyes. "She said, 'Don't give up. Mother and Jill are here and they're OK. Whatever you do, don't commit suicide. Don't give up.'"

He continued to talk about his sister and what he felt about the experience until the end of that session.

In the next session, Christopher reported what some others who have IADCs report: He had experienced a spontaneous ADC during sleep, two nights before the current session. In the ADC, his father was begging him for forgiveness, and his two deceased sisters were in the background. But his father was in a dark area and his two sisters were standing in a bright area smiling at him. He said his sisters then came forward and said, "Let it go and forgive him. Forgive him for yourself. Not for him, but for you." His fear woke him and the ADC ended.

Christopher had the sense that his two sisters were there to help him forgive his father, as though they were figuratively holding hands with Christopher.

I asked him whether he was willing to do an IADC with his father as the focus. He said, "Yes. I feel like I have to do it now."

I had to begin with some eye movements to reduce the fear he felt from the prospect of confronting his father. The fear increased as he faced it, and successive eye movements brought it down. Then his anger went up dramatically, and after three sets of eye movements, started coming back down. With that, I was able to use core-focused EMDR to address the core sadness, which was a more generalized sadness for his two sisters and himself.

When the sadness peaked and started to come back down, I administered a final set of eye movements and the IADC began. Christopher reported that his father was there.

"At first I pushed him away," he explained, after opening his eyes. "I couldn't stand to even be around him. I looked at him and it felt so strange. My father looked very worried. I had a real strong feeling he knew how much he had hurt me and my sisters. I felt like he was really sorry and that's the first time I've ever, ever felt that with him.

"Then I asked him, 'Why? Why did you do all that to us?' I heard him as clearly as I can hear you; he kept saying 'I'm sorry, I'm sorry, I'm sorry.' You know, I feel like he really was sorry. He said it was no excuse, but he acted that way because that's the way his father treated him. I can't feel great about what he did, but I really feel different, like I can forgive him."

When Christopher came for the next session, he said he had had a very strange dream as he was half asleep the previous evening. "It scared the shit out of me," he said, but he meant it literally. He saw his father's drunken buddies in the dream, and filled his pants out of fear.

I did the IADC procedure using the images to get at the fear. After the fear diminished, I induced another IADC. He reported that his two sisters appeared and reassured him that the images of the men would not come back again. "I could feel the love they have for me. I'll tell you as truly as I can, they touched me and hugged me. I could feel it."

Christopher's feelings were too intense to go away in two or three sessions, but he said they were dramatically improved. After several more sessions, the intrusive memories, nightmares, and thoughts of suicide had ended.

Forgiving heals.

Feeling Forgiven by the Deceased Heals Guilt

Patients often feel guilt because of deep-seated feelings that they did something to the deceased or didn't do something they should have done. Because they are unable to talk through the issues with the deceased, the guilt lingers. It intensifies as other issues exacerbate the survivor's condition, such as conflicts with family members.

In the IADCs I have induced, patients always perceive the deceased forgiving them for transgressions or omissions, regardless of the number of years the survivors have been convinced that the deceased could not forgive them.

Linda's Case: "Grandma said 'I love you, Linda,' and I said, 'I love you too, Grandma.' I could feel her love for me."

Linda's immediate family had not been part of her life while she was growing up, so her grandmother had become her mother, father, and companion through her childhood and adult life. The two had no other family relationships. The love they shared was deep and committed.

With her grandmother's encouragement, Linda grew into a successful professional, traveling extensively and sharing her experiences with her grandmother after each trip. Linda was in Europe when she received the call that her grandmother had suddenly fallen gravely ill. She took the next plane home, rushing to the hospital. But when she arrived, she was too late. Her grandmother had passed away.

Inconsolable, she turned her grief into self-blame: "I wasn't there when she needed me most." Nothing could turn her away from her dark, inward tumble into depression.

Linda came to me for a different issue, but it became clear as we talked that guilt was consuming her. She believed her grandmother had died a lonely, painful death and she was to blame. She wasn't there at the one time in her life when her grandmother had needed her. Now nothing could be done. She was sure her beloved grandmother felt Linda had abandoned her.

As we talked, it became clear to me that having an IADC with her grandmother would allow her to resolve the guilt feelings. After a brief explanation of IADCs, she was skeptical, but agreed to the procedure.

I completed the procedure and the IADC began. Linda closed her eyes and sat stoically; then her expression changed. She began describing what she was seeing: "I see Grandma, but she's young and healthy." Linda was immersed in the experience, forgetting her earlier skepticism. "She's thoroughly content and happy." She paused and opened her eyes. "She told me she died peacefully in her sleep, that I must not feel guilty about anything." Linda wept with happiness.

I continued the session with her, taking her back into the IADC. Afterward, through smiles and tears, she explained, "I also felt her real presence; it was more than just words. Grandma said 'I love you, Linda,' and I said, 'I love you too, Grandma.' I could feel her love for me."

Linda looked at me as though I would be amazed by the remarkable experience. I smiled and encouraged her to continue. "She said she was proud of me, and happy about the changes I just made in my life. Dr. Botkin, she mentioned things that have happened to me since her death. She's really been with me."

The session ended with Linda feeling a joyful sense of reconnection with her grandmother. She was deeply moved by the experience and all of her feelings of guilt and sadness had vanished.

Mark's Case: "I heard them, very clearly, say they had been waiting to hear what I had to say, and they forgive me."

Mark is another patient whose guilt was resolved when he felt forgiven by the deceased. In his case, the deceased were members of an entire family.

Mark walked slowly into my office for his first psychotherapy session and slumped into the chair. I had no idea how heavy a burden he was carrying on his sagging shoulders until he explained what had happened.

Nearly 25 years before, he had been embarking on a successful professional career when his life had changed in an instant. Driving alone one night, he was blinded momentarily by car lights and drifted into the path of a car carrying a mother, father, and their 12-year-old daughter. The collision killed the family, although Mark was uninjured. He was charged in the case, found guilty, and sentenced to years of probation.

From the day of the accident onward, he awoke every morning to deep sadness and severe guilt, plodding through each day, reliving the accident over and over in his mind. He became depressed, attempted suicide twice, watched two marriages fail, and was on the verge of losing his job because of his depressive behavior and alcohol abuse.

Mark was convinced that he was destined to suffer for the rest of his life. There was no way to undo what had happened, and he couldn't feel forgiven by the only people from whom forgiving words would matter— the young family that had died.

He ended his story in tears, shaking his head. Life had ended, he felt, even though he was still walking through it.

He agreed to let me help him understand and deal with his grief with IADC therapy. I performed the IADC procedure and he sat quietly with his eyes closed. After a moment, he said, "I can see them. It's the family with the little girl. They're standing together and smiling. . . . God, they look happy and peaceful. They're very happy being together and they're telling me they really like where they are."

Mark had never seen the family. Because of his emotional suffering over the incident, he had refused to look at newspapers in which the family was pictured. But even though he had never seen them or heard descriptions of them, he was sure it was them.

"I can see each one very clearly, and especially the girl. She's standing in front of the mom and dad. She has short red hair, freckles, and a wonderful smile. I can see the dad walking around, like he's showing me how he can walk. I have the feeling from him that he had multiple sclerosis before he died, and he is really happy he can now move around freely."

After a few moments, Mark opened his eyes. "I told them I was very sorry about what had happened and said I felt very sad. And then I heard them, very clearly, say they had been waiting to hear what I had to say, and then they forgave me."

Marked paused, overcome by the experience. He looked at me and said, "I didn't make all of this up. It came to me as clearly as I'm looking at you right now. I didn't imagine it; I couldn't have imagined it." He shook his head slowly. "I feel like a huge burden has been lifted off of me."

He said he was worried that I would think he was crazy. What happened was beyond anything he had ever experienced. "They were really there," he insisted.

I reassured him that what had happened to him was something I had seen many times before.

As he was leaving, he shook my hand and said, "I feel great!"

But the next day, I received a phone call from Mark saying he had to see me right away. He was in my office within an hour, explaining what had happened since our session. "I never could look at the newspaper reports after the accident. I couldn't look at any pictures of the accident or people and wouldn't let anyone tell me anything about them. My sister kept clippings of everything, but I could never look at them. Then, yesterday, I was feeling so much better, so I stopped by my sister's house and asked her to get out the old clippings of the accident. She showed them to me, including one color picture of the family, and I freaked out. The girl had short red hair, freckles, and the same wonderful smile I saw in my vision of them yesterday. It was her!

"But that's not all. One article said that the man had severe multiple sclerosis and had been in a wheelchair for years before he died!"

Mark's life changed from that moment. Today, all issues pertaining to the accident remain resolved, and he reports dramatically improved relationships with people who are important to him.

Getting Advice from the Deceased Helps Resolve Anger and Guilt

Sometimes, patients report that they have received advice from the deceased about issues that have caused them to feel angry or guilty. In all cases, the advice is specific and relevant, and it resolves the anger and guilt.

George's Case: His brother told him he was on the right track by seeking help for his problems and changing his lifestyle.

George and his younger brother had entered a life of drugs and crime together many years before he came to see me. In the course of their dealings, they developed some enemies who vowed revenge on them. One day, George went to his brother's apartment and found his brother severely beaten and unconscious. When medical personnel arrived, they pronounced him dead.

In addition to feeling a tremendous sense of loss, George believed he was ultimately responsible for his brother's death. To make matters worse, when George told his mother that her son was dead, his mother screamed at George that if it weren't for him, his brother would still be alive. George also felt intense rage at those who had killed his brother. Over the years, especially during times he felt the loss most deeply, he continued to have thoughts of revenge.

George had no trouble going into an IADC. He said he saw his brother "happy and very peaceful" and felt that he "connected" with him. He reported that his brother had a lot of advice for him. He told him that seeking revenge for his death would ruin George's life and that he should let his anger go. George reported that his brother told him that he shouldn't feel guilty, that he was responsible for making his own choices and he had learned from his mistakes. George said his brother also told him he was on the right track by seeking help for his problems and changing his lifestyle.

George's feelings of sadness, guilt, and anger fully resolved during his IADC. He recommitted himself to his goal of moving on and making a better life for himself. In a later session, George said that he felt physically better than he had in many years. The extreme bodily tension he had felt for years prior to the session had decreased dramatically.

Life Reviews and Troubled Lives

In IADCs, the deceased who had lived troubled lives are consistently experienced as taking full responsibility for their behavior while alive. Frequently, the patients also report the deceased as saying they have learned from their mistakes and are eager to help those who are still living. They seem to have been through a life review. They are remorseful, take responsibility for their behavior, and understand how their behavior affected others.

None of those who had been cruel in life or had otherwise hurt those around them appeared in a hellish place, although experiencers often describe them as being in a dark area. This issue will be further addressed in chapter 13.

11

IADCs with Combat Veterans: Making Peace with War

Forgive thy enemy, be reconciled to him, give him assistance . . .
—Confucius

The experience of forgiveness our patients report in the IADCs reduces or eliminates the feelings of guilt. The forgiveness felt by combat veterans for killing the enemy or civilians, or surviving when their fellow soldiers had perished, are special cases of this remarkable transformation resulting from feeling forgiven or being given permission to stop feeling guilty.

At our post-traumatic stress disorder unit, we treated combat veterans from WWII, the Korean War, the Vietnam War, and Desert Storm. After working with a few thousand combat veterans, I can say that I did not meet one veteran who was psychologically ready to kill another human being as a result of basic and advanced training. The soldier will kill readily only after being sufficiently traumatized in combat to develop feelings of rage that allow him to dehumanize the enemy, making killing psychologically acceptable. When a new soldier displays rage in response to a traumatic event, the soldier's comrades feel the new soldier can be trusted. The rage covers up, however, the most distressing and painful core emotions: fear and intense sadness. Sadness and paralyzing fear are not acceptable in combat and have little survival value.

Most of the problems my colleagues and I saw appeared later in the veterans' lives. Frequently, their anger dropped off as they aged, baring the intense sadness and guilt that anger had covered up. As the anger decreased, it became increasingly difficult to dehumanize the enemy. Then the rage thoughts ("I'm glad I killed those bastards. I wish I could have killed more of them.") were often replaced by feelings of guilt and sadness ("I was wrong for killing them. They too had feelings and families who loved them.").

The look of fear in the eyes of the enemy before he died became the face of a family man who never saw his children grow up. The memory of a civilian the soldier killed that was covered by layers of anger during the war often surfaced in later life as nightmares about an innocent human being who suffered for no reason.

The resulting guilt and sadness were so overwhelming and debilitating that many of our veterans chose to maintain their anger for the rest of their lives. Ultimately, however, for the combat veteran to make peace with himself and shed his anger and guilt, he had to confront and work through the sadness at the core. Thus, these veterans needed to grieve not only the deaths of their comrades, but also of those they killed.

The wonderful news for us on the unit was that if a veteran was willing to allow the EMDR process to take him beyond the anger and guilt to work through the deep sadness, the anger and guilt would often immediately vanish, even though those emotions were not directly addressed. Anger and guilt psychologically protected them from experiencing the more painful core issue of sadness. Guilt that was not resolved along with the sadness was routinely addressed spontaneously in the IADC.

I discovered that the IADC process is the same for combat veterans as it is for someone who has lost a family member through death. The combat veterans had a more complex mixture of guilt, anger, regret, sadness, and traumatic symptoms, but they entered the IADC experience just as easily and just as deeply as people who did not have the combat trauma. As with civilian cases, the goal was to process the core sadness, which then allowed the experiencer to enter a receptive state.

The following combat cases illustrate the effects of IADCs on the men we treated who were suffering combat-related traumatic grief.

Mike's Case: "He communicated to me that he is very content where he is, and he understands that I had to do what I did."

Mike arrived in Vietnam a few days before his first major battle. The battle went on for some time, and when his unit started running low on ammunition, Mike was intensely afraid they were all going to die. Just when it appeared that all hope had faded, a helicopter arrived with supplies. As they were unloading boxes of ammunition, Mike looked up and saw a young enemy VC running toward them. He could see his face clearly. Overcome with intense anger, he shot and killed the young man.

Even though it was the first time he had killed another human being, he felt exhilarated and in control of his fate. When the battle was over, the other soldiers congratulated Mike, and he felt that they fully trusted and accepted him. He didn't think much more about the event for the remainder of his tour.

When he returned home, however, Mike experienced nightmares about the event that continued for the next 35 years. He repeatedly saw the face of the young VC he had killed and began to wonder how old this man was and whether he had a family that grieved his death. At times, he could retrieve his combat anger to justify the incident, but at other times he felt great remorse and sadness.

"I just feel terrible. What I did goes against everything I have ever believed," he said to me in my office. It was clear that Mike needed to confront his sadness by fully grieving the death of the person he had killed.

When we used EMDR to address his sadness directly, it increased until it peaked, then began to subside. At that point, I administered the IADC procedure until the IADC began. With his eyes still closed on the second induction, he began to describe what he saw. "I can see him, the guy I killed, but it doesn't look like the face I saw in Nam and what I see in my nightmares. I see him smiling and happy." Mike sat quietly for a moment, then opened his eyes. "He communicated to me that he is very content where he is, and he understands that I had to do what I did."

After a few minutes of describing what had happened, he ended by saying, "I'm really surprised the guy would feel that way. Really strange. I feel like him and me aren't just OK with each other; I feel like we have a special bond."

After that session, the look on the young man's face before he died that had haunted Mike for over 35 years was replaced by the smiling and happy face he experienced in his IADC. He told me at the end of the session, "I'm trying to remember the old face I always saw in my nightmares, but I can't."

A two-year follow-up revealed that Mike's nightmares about the incident had vanished from that day, and he felt only "an important connection" to the man he had killed.

George's Case: "I didn't know dead people have a sense of humor."

George came to me because he had been plagued by feelings of guilt for decades. When he was in Vietnam, his job was to be the driver for a major, chauffeuring him anyplace he wanted to go in a jeep. One afternoon, George was helping with another project, so a substitute driver took over the job of driving the major. As they drove down a road, the jeep ran over a 500-pound land mine and both the major and substitute driver were killed instantly.

When George heard the news, he felt great sadness at first, then tremendous guilt that another soldier had died when he should have been driving the jeep.

When he finished telling me the story, I did an IADC induction and, on the third set of eye movements, he closed his eyes, sat quietly a few seconds, then laughed lightly. When he finally opened his eyes, he described his experience.

"I saw the guy who was driving the jeep for me. I got the message from him that he was saying 'It's OK.' Then he cracked a joke. He said, 'I'm one of your stressors.'" When the vets fill out paperwork about their physical and psychological condition, they describe traumas, called "stressors." They receive an additional percentage of their normal payment based on the severity and effect of the stressor.

"He said to me, 'I'm the reason you're getting 30%,' and he laughed. I didn't know dead people have a sense of humor."

George's guilt and sadness over the death of the substitute driver resolved during that session. In a follow-up weeks later, he said he still felt none of the guilt and sadness that had affected him for years, and he still laughed when he thought about what the soldier had said to him.

George was then enthusiastic about the IADC process. Many of those who experience it want to use the process to experience other people who have passed away. George said he'd like to IADC his cousin, an officer who had died in Vietnam very soon after arriving, but George wasn't sure how he died. He said, "Maybe he'll come through and let me know how he died." I agreed to do the induction, partly out of curiosity, but mostly because I thought it would help George.

We went through the normal induction and he closed his eyes. After a few seconds, he opened his eyes and told me what had happened. "I saw him right away and he hugged me. Then he told me something that surprised me. He said he had been fragged. I didn't know that."

What George was referring to was the common occurrence of officers being killed by their own men with fragmentation grenades. Some officers went through 90 days of training and were immediately shipped to Vietnam, where some would start ordering the seasoned combat veterans into dangerous situations because they didn't know what they were doing. The soldiers called them "90-day wonders." These green officers often got their men killed because of their lack of experience.

Out in the field, with no witnesses, sometimes the 90-day wonders were fragged by their own men who were fed up with being put in dangerous situations by an officer who didn't know what he was doing. Although George received information that would under other circumstances be very disturbing to him, the peaceful feeling he experienced during his IADC seemed to completely overcome any negative thoughts or feelings.

Tucker's Case: "If we can forgive you, then surely you can forgive yourself."

Tucker's case is an example of the patient being forgiven for acts that may seem unforgivable.

He told me, haltingly, the story of what had happened, at times unable to continue because of his sobs. He was nearing the end of his tour in Vietnam and had suffered many losses in the 11 months he was there. He saw his friends blown to pieces, watched them dying in the hospital, and saw the Vietnamese civilians carry bombs into groups of American soldiers and detonate them. After 11 months of horror, he was full of rage. The rage insulated him, as it did all the other soldiers, from the intense grief, fear, and remorse he would have felt without it.

On Tucker's last mission, his unit was ordered to destroy an enemy village. While in the village, Tucker and two other soldiers went into one of the hooches (huts) and spotted an old man and a boy sitting beside guns lying on the floor, but they had their hands up to surrender. Tucker flew into a full-blown rage and shot them. At the time, he felt only rage.

When he walked out of the village, however, the look of fear on the faces of the old man and young boy before they died began to bother him. A month later, he left Vietnam, but the memories stayed with him and increased in intensity. For 30 years, Tucker had been tormented daily by intrusive images of their faces and reliving the event. He had made two serious suicide attempts in the previous three years.

When Tucker finished, he cried, with his face in his hands.

Tucker had already experienced an IADC involving a different incident. That session had fully resolved his grief over the incident. He had carried such overwhelming guilt and shame about these killings, however, that he hadn't brought them up until this session, and he was reluctant to have an induction because he was sure the old man and boy would be angry with him. He felt he couldn't stand that because he was already consumed with guilt.

He nevertheless decided to go through with the IADC. "I guess I'll take whatever I have coming," he said. "It couldn't be any worse than how I'm feeling now."

We went through the core-focused EMDR procedure and his sadness increased. He was wracked with sobs and slid out of his chair onto the floor from the intense remorse he felt over the pain he had caused the old man and boy. I quickly gave him more eye movements to reduce the sadness until he was at the point where I knew he was ready for the receptive state necessary for an IADC. He closed his eyes and sat quietly for a minute. Suddenly he opened his eyes and described to me what had happened. "I saw the old man. He stood there looking very peaceful and said to me, 'Why were you so angry?' I couldn't handle it, so I opened my eyes."

I asked, "Do you have an answer?"

He said, "Yes. About a week before we went into the village, my squad went missing. We went out searching the next day and found their bodies. We could see that they had been tortured before they were killed. I was madder than I've ever been. I ran into the brush looking for someone to kill. I vowed I would have my revenge."

"Tell him that."

Tucker looked at me apprehensively, then said, "OK. Let's do it."

I did another set of eye movements with him and he closed his eyes. After a few seconds, he opened them and said, "I told him. But it was like he already knew it. He smiled and said he could understand it because he knew my 'heart was crying.' He told me he forgives me. Then the young boy appeared. He said he understood my pain too, and he also forgives me."

Tucker still looked troubled. I asked him what was wrong. He said, "Maybe they can forgive me, but I can't forgive myself."

I said, "Keep that thought in mind and let's do another set of eye movements. Stay with the thought."

I administered another set of eye movements and he closed his eyes. When he opened them, he said, "They told me, 'If we can forgive you, then surely you can forgive yourself.' I guess I really feel they are at peace and happy, so I can let it go."

Tucker did let it go and reported that he felt like the issue was finally resolved. A two-year follow-up revealed that none of the intrusive symptoms associated with this memory had returned.

Eric's Case: "I can see the boy playing and laughing in a beautiful field with rolling hills, trees, and grass."

One of the great horrors of war is that civilians, especially children, are caught up in the cruelty, violence, and death. In the Vietnam War, young children were strapped with explosives and told to go to a group of American soldiers and detonate them, killing themselves and the soldiers. Americans soon learned the danger signals when a child approached with the bulges that likely were explosives hidden under the child's clothing. Unfortunately, at times that meant the boy or girl would either be killed by an alert American soldier or die in the explosion, taking Americans' lives.

That was the situation Eric experienced, and the result was an image that gave him nightmares and intrusive thoughts for years after the war.

Eric had been in Vietnam only a few weeks when he and a group of American soldiers spotted a Vietnamese boy at some distance running toward them. Eric noticed that his more experienced partner did not take his eyes off the boy. When the boy got to about 30 feet from them, Eric's partner lifted his rifle and shot at the boy, hitting the explosives concealed under his clothing. There was a huge explosion and the boy was killed instantly. The boy had been on a suicide mission to kill the group of American soldiers. Eric's partner knew that if he didn't shoot, they would all die.

For many years after the war, Eric suffered from uncontrollable, intrusive thoughts and nightmares about the incident. I began therapy with him at the VA hospital to alleviate his suffering.

After I explained the IADC procedure to him, Eric protested that he did not believe in an afterlife, but said he was willing to give the procedure a try anyway. I did some preliminary EMDR, ending with a set of eye movements to help him enter a receptive state. When no IADC resulted, I repeated the induction process and the IADC began without difficulty.

"I can see the boy playing and laughing in a beautiful field with rolling hills, trees, and grass," he said. "It's lush beyond description. There's a very peaceful feeling there."

He opened his eyes and said, "I'll tell you, I was really surprised to see him in one piece, without any injuries. I really don't know what to make out of this." Eric ended the session by saying that he did not interpret what happened in spiritual terms or as evidence of an afterlife.

An eight-month follow-up revealed that all of his intrusive symptoms associated with the incident had disappeared and his grief was resolved. He also continued to be confused about his experience. "I guess the mind can do some pretty weird things," he said.

It became apparent to us from Eric's experience and others like his that neither the patient's prior beliefs nor subsequent beliefs have any effect on the IADC experience or the outcome of the experience. In other words, it appears that the experience itself, not the interpretation of it, is responsible for resolution of the grief and associated symptoms.

Terry's Case: "I'm very sorry we did it, but I feel close to them and believe they really are OK and they forgive me."

Some of our vets came out of Desert Storm. Like Vietnam, the war was especially difficult because friendlies and the enemy were intermingled. That resulted in an event that created intrusive memories for Terry, one of my vets.

Terry and a few other soldiers went into an underground bunker not knowing who was in there. That was always a tense situation because they didn't know where the enemy might hide in the darkness. Terry and the others with him were on edge, ready to kill any enemy as soon as they were spotted before they could get off a shot.

Terry was first into the bunker. He had his rifle in firing position, pointed into the area illuminated by his flashlight. He made a left turn and very quietly stepped into an open area. Suddenly, his light shined on Iraqis. He opened fire immediately. The other soldiers rushed in and opened fire as well. They discovered that they had killed four Iraqis.

It wasn't until after the heat of that reflex response that he realized the Iraqis all had a look of surprise on their faces and no weapons. As they walked out of the bunker, the other guys congratulated Terry for his quick response. They sat outside, talking about what happened, but began to realize they weren't sure if they were Iraqi enemies or friendlies.

Six months later, he was home from Desert Storm, but the question of whether they had killed friendlies never left him. He was very worried that they had killed four innocent civilians taking shelter from the firefights outside.

He told me the story matter-of-factly, but I knew that he wouldn't have brought it up if it hadn't been bothering him. He agreed to try to get in touch with his feelings about the situation. I began the core-focused EMDR to take him directly to his core sadness. As I did, he began to weep softly and said the sadness had increased to "a 9 or 10."

The sadness then began to come down. I gave him another set of eye movements, asked him to close his eyes, and said, "Just go with whatever happens."

After a couple of minutes, he opened his eyes. He shook his head and looked at me. "I saw them. They told me they were friendlies, but they smiled at me and were very forgiving. I don't speak Iraqi, but I wasn't hearing words. I just knew what they were saying. 'We're OK. We're doing fine. It's OK.'"

"How do you feel about that?" I asked.

"I'm very sorry we did it, but I feel close to them and believe that they really are OK and that they forgive me."

Terry's IADC gave him a message he didn't want to hear, as many IADCs do. His issues resolved, however, because of his perception that his victims forgave him and were OK.

12

Requirements for a Successful IADC

The way out of grief is through it.

—Bob Deits, *Life after Loss*

Given the fact that core-focused EMDR and the IADC procedure both require that the patient is open and willing at every step in the procedure, it is remarkable that so many people are able to walk down the path to a successful IADC. That is testimony to the remarkable therapeutic power of core-focused EMDR and the IADC.

Some people, however, are not able to experience an IADC even though we use the same procedure that engenders IADCs in others. We now have some understanding of the conditions that must be present for a successful IADC, and we have tentative explanations for why some people have difficulty.

A 98 Percent IADC Rate on the PTSD Unit, but 70 Percent Elsewhere

Patients more consistently had IADCs in the post-traumatic stress disorder (PTSD) unit of the VA hospital where I practiced than they have had in private practice sessions. The rate of induction was about 98 percent of all patients in the PTSD unit. In other words, it was the rare patient who did not have an IADC.

These seem to be the unique conditions at the VA hospital that resulted in more IADCs:

1. The patients did not come to have an IADC and thus had no anticipation or preconceived expectations for the experience. Many, in fact, insisted it wouldn't work for them.

2. The patients trusted the psychotherapists and were willing to relax into a receptive state.

3. Since the patients lived on an inpatient unit for the duration of treatment, current-life stressors and distractions were kept to a minimum.

Outside of that VA hospital environment, people who have come to us for grief therapy and IADCs seem to have around a 70 percent success rate, but this tentative figure is based on a much smaller population of subjects. Many of those who have not succeeded in having an IADC have come with high expectations for the experience, a factor virtually not present in the PTSD unit. Some of the people who hear about IADCs and wish to experience one are interested because they have read about NDEs and ADCs and have an expectation about what they believe they should experience. The preconceptions and expectations appear to inhibit the IADC from unfolding.

The 70 percent success rate is based on a two 90-minute session model that I follow when doing IADC therapy. Some of my colleagues have suggested to me that my success rate would be much higher if I saw these patients for a greater number of sessions.

If the person in any way strains to make the IADC happen or to influence the direction of the IADC, it will not occur or will stop when the subject tries to take control. Someone trying to experience preconceived scenarios about the IADC will have difficulty entering a receptive mood in which they allow anything to happen spontaneously, without expectations or attempting to impose their beliefs.

Conditions Unnecessary and Those Necessary to Induce IADCs

After several thousand IADCs, we can make generalizations about the conditions that do not seem to be necessary for a successful IADC and those that seem to be necessary.

Unnecessary Conditions

We know that having an IADC does *not* depend on these conditions:

1. **Special mental faculties.** Those who have had IADCs do not appear to be in a different population from those who do not. Some have speculated that PTSD may predispose one to the experience, but the presence or absence of trauma in my private patients appears to make no difference.

2. **A belief system.** Successful IADCs have been experienced by atheists, agnostics, Christians, Muslims, Jews, Buddhists, and people from a variety of other religious and spiritual persuasions. If the person expects to have an IADC that matches stereotypic images from their religion, however, that will inhibit the natural unfolding of the IADC.

3. **Suggestions from the psychotherapist.** We have discovered that psychotherapists who try to blend the IADC induction with their own more leading forms of therapy virtually eliminate the incidence of IADCs in their patients. For example, some therapists who are comfortable with hypnosis have attempted to use subtle suggestion to induce the experience. That actually prevents it from occurring. The psychotherapist must actively step back from the process and allow the IADC to occur without hindrance or guidance.

4. **Intense grief.** IADCs occur in people with modest, residual grief as well as those in deep psychological pain from intrusive memories and deep sadness.

Necessary Conditions

The procedure that results in the IADC *does* seem to require the following:

1. **Willingness.** The patient must be willing to go through core-focused EMDR therapy and fully access his or her sadness. Patients who are still experiencing shock and numbing may not be ready to access core issues fully.

2. **Receptivity.** Foremost, the IADC requires an open, receptive attitude. After sadness and the attendant emotions begin to decrease, the psychotherapist instructs the patient to "Be open to anything that happens" and administers another set of eye movements. The patient must then be open to any experience that occurs by minimizing his or her expectations and beliefs about the experience. This attitude results from both the therapist and patient letting go at the right moment in the process. Neither tries to direct the experience. The IADC takes over and unfolds naturally and effortlessly. If the therapist or patient tries to make it fulfill a set of expectations, the IADC will not occur.

The Therapist Must Follow the IADC Procedure Precisely

The sequence is critical to the IADC. It begins by diminishing the intensity of the sadness. As long as the therapist and patient remain focused on anger and guilt, the sadness remains buried. Core-focused EMDR uncovers the sadness and patients typically address it fully for the first time. After they face the sadness and it starts to lose its intensity, the primary distracting emotion has been set aside. Sometimes other traumatic and intrusive factors need to be reduced as well. Another set of eye movements then increases the receptive psychological state that allows the patient's own sense of reconnection to resolve the grief.

This is the critical procedure:

1. The patient must go through core-focused EMDR therapy and fully access his or her sadness. I inform patients prior to the procedure that if they are not yet ready to access their sadness fully, the procedure won't work.

2. After sadness and attendant traumatic intrusions begin to decrease, the psychotherapist instructs the patient to "Be open to anything that happens" and administers another set of eye movements.

3. The IADC unfolds naturally.

Deviating from the sequence reduces the chances that the patient will have an IADC. We have also found that patients who begin to have an IADC, but then attempt to alter it or make it occur differently, interrupt the natural unfolding and the IADC stops or comes haltingly. For example, in one IADC, the patient heard his deceased daughter calling, "Dad, Dad," and the patient started to search for her in his mental imagery. That stopped the IADC from happening and he was not able to relax back into the receptive mode he had at the beginning of the experience. He was too intent on having the experience.

Intense Grief Is Not Necessary to Have the Experience

Many patients have successful IADCs decades after a death or involving a person for whom the patient never had strong grief. As a result, they have little grief at the time of the IADC. That fact strongly suggests that those having IADCs are not experiencing grief hallucinations; they may have little or no grief. Intense grief is not a satisfactory explanation for the IADC experience.

Ileene's Case: "I had a real feeling of talking with Grandma."

Ileene was very close to her grandmother. When she had died over 40 years before, Ileene, who believed in an afterlife, began to have occasional thoughts about where she was and how she was doing. When she came to see me for another issue and learned about IADCs, she asked me to do an IADC to help her find out how her grandmother was doing. She explained that she was feeling no grief now because the death was so far in the past. The core-focused EMDR revealed that she was correct; she had very little residual sadness.

I induced Ileene's IADC on the second try without difficulty in spite of the minimal amount of sadness. While her eyes were closed, Ileene reported that she saw her grandmother. "She's looking very happy and peaceful, standing in a bright area with white light all around her. She looks younger and healthier than she did during the years before she died."

Ileene was quiet for a few seconds, then opened her eyes. "I told her, 'I love you' and Grandma said, 'I know you do, and I love you too.' Then she faded away."

Ileene was ecstatic about her experience: "I had a real feeling of talking with Grandma," she said. "It was very real."

The Patient's Beliefs Have No Effect on the Healing That Results from Nearly All IADCs

A patient's belief system does not influence the success of the IADC. People who have had successful IADCs include adherents to all the major religions and spiritual practices as well as agnostics and atheists. Some are convinced they have witnessed a real, imminent afterlife; others believe they have had an unusual mental event the brain must have conjured up. Regardless of their conclusions about the source, however, all are healed of their grief during the IADC session.

Bernard's Case: "I want you to be happy because I'm happy."

Bernard was a successful corporate executive who had it all. An MBA graduate, he had been assured he was on the verge of further advancements in his firm. His wife cared for their three young children while he climbed the corporate ladder.

Then, ten years before he came to see me, tragedy took it all away, bringing him to suicidal depression. Bernard, his wife, and their three children were returning from a Christmas party when a speeding car coming from the opposite direction rammed them head on. He described the horrible scene to me. "I remember being in and out of consciousness, with red flashing lights and blood everywhere. I could hear my children screaming. I passed out and woke in the hospital. Then they told me. My wife, Margie, and little Brent were dead. Angie, my daughter, was paralyzed. I was told I probably had some brain damage. Only our other daughter was not hurt much." He was visibly shaken as he spoke.

I asked him whether he would be willing to have an IADC and he said he didn't believe in that kind of thing, but would do it because he was desperate for relief. I used EMDR to reduce the intrusive images he had of the bloody scene and screams of his children. I then used core-focused EMDR to access and reduce his sadness and began the IADC induction process. On the third try, the IADC began.

He described what happened. "I can see Margie holding Brent." He smiled. "They look healthy and so happy together." He opened his eyes.

"They told me they are very concerned about my pain. Margie said, 'We are OK. You need to be OK too so you can take care of our children.'"

Bernard's grief appeared to be completely resolved at the end of the session, in spite of his skepticism. Later that week, he called me saying he had been feeling depressed about the fact that his deceased son never had a chance to live a full life. "Then, last night," he told me, "I had a vivid dream. Brent came to me and said, 'I love you, Dad. I want you to be happy because I'm happy.' I finally felt at peace."

I asked him if he believed he had actually experienced a real connection with his deceased wife and son. He answered, "No, I don't believe in that stuff. I think my mind has just convinced me that it's OK for me to get on with my life so I can take care of my children."

In my follow-up two years later, I learned that Bernard's grief had remained completely resolved. He had gone back to work and was doing very well while caring for his two children.

Bernard's case is one of dozens I have witnessed in which the patient does not believe anything will happen, is not expecting something to happen, and may deny that the experience was a real communication, but the grief is resolved as fully as it is for someone who believes he or she has had an actual experience of reconnection with the deceased.

A Native American Patient's Case: "You know, what my elders taught me was wrong."

In one case, a Native American patient expressed concern about having an IADC experience because he had been taught by his elders that after death the soul divides into two parts, one good and one bad, and only the bad part communicates with the living.

We went through the IADC induction process and he experienced the same loving, positive reconnection with his loved ones all IADC experiencers do. Afterward, he said to me, "You know, what my elders taught me was wrong. I know that now."

This patient's belief system did not alter the consistently positive nature of the IADCs.

Greg's Patient's Case: "What, that talking-to-the-dead crap?"

In another case, Greg Rimoldi, the IADC psychotherapist and colleague mentioned previously, had a successful IADC with a patient that illustrates the fact that the patient's beliefs before or after the IADC do not inhibit the healing power of the IADC. At the patient's next session after the successful IADC, Greg asked the patient whether he would like to IADC someone else. The patient remarked, "What, that talking-to-the-dead crap? Nope."

Greg was a little nonplussed at the remark because the patient's successful IADC seemed to resolve a trauma the patient had relived for years. He assumed that perhaps the trauma was not resolved after all, so he asked about it.

"Well, would you like to work on that trauma again?"

"Nope," the patient responded. "Don't need to."

The patient's belief system told him the IADC was "crap," but his trauma and grief had been healed by it; the patient's belief system had nothing to do with the success of the IADC.

Cases in Which Patients Were Initially Not Fully Receptive

Jean's case is an example of what happens when the patient tries to control the IADC.

Jean's Case: She tried to look at her intently to get a clearer picture, but her mother's image faded away.

Jean was nine years old when her mother died during heart surgery. For the two years before her mother's death, Jean realized that something was wrong, but the family didn't tell her that her mother was under treatment for a serious heart condition. Jean's father worked, so when her mother was hospitalized from time to time, Jean, an only child, would stay with neighbors. She told me she remembered it being a very scary and confusing time for her.

One day, Jean and her father visited her mother in the hospital. Her mother said she was going to have surgery the next day, but everything would be fine. The next day when Jean came home from school, the minister and her father were standing in the living room. Her father sat down with her and said, "Mom has gone to Heaven, Jean."

Jean was inconsolable and felt that, in the 38 years since that day, she had not fully recovered from the shock. I explained the IADC procedure to her and she agreed to try it. The usual induction process resulted in a dramatic increase in sadness before her IADC began.

After the induction, she closed her eyes for a few seconds, then opened her eyes and reported that she saw her mother standing in a field, far away, "next to a bunch of trees." She tried to look at her intently to get a clearer picture, but her mother's image faded away.

I told her that the IADC unfolds naturally and that she shouldn't try to make it happen. She just needed to relax and accept whatever happened. "Let the experience come to you," I told her.

I did another induction and she sat quietly. When she opened her eyes, she told me she had seen her mother again, but this time much closer. She saw the same background that was in the first IADC: a beautiful field and leafy trees, all a rich green. She explained that she stayed relaxed and spoke to her mother. "I miss you and love you," she said. Her mother said, "I miss and love you, too. Enjoy your children. Everything is OK."

Jean smiled at me and said with quiet assertion, "I don't *think* that was my mother; I *know* it was." She left the session that day saying she felt an overwhelming sense of peace for the first time in 38 years.

Larry's case was similar. He had strong expectations for the IADC that actually thwarted it repeatedly. But when he relaxed and allowed it to be whatever it would be, the IADC unfolded naturally, in ways the patient could not anticipate.

Larry's Case: He told his father that he loved him, and his father said, "I know you do, and I love you too."

Larry was in his late twenties when his father developed heart problems. He flew home to visit his father, but after a week, his father's medical condition appeared to improve, so he flew back home. Larry described his family as very close, but they were emotionally reserved and never openly expressed or talked about feelings. Larry was surprised when one day he received a letter in which his father warmly expressed his love for him.

Two days later, as Larry was responding to the letter, he received a phone call telling him his father had died. Larry speculated that his father wrote the letter because he sensed that death was imminent. For nearly 20 years, Larry had been privately tormented by the fact that he had not had a chance to respond to his father's letter telling him that he loved him. His eyes filled with tears as he talked about his unfinished business with his father.

Larry was not the typical induction patient because, even though he had never had an NDE or ADC and knew very little about such experiences, he was enthusiastic and believed that the procedure would work. He based his confidence on his Christian belief in life after death.

When he told me about his expectations of having a spiritual experience as he envisioned it, I instructed him to put his expectations about the experience on hold as well as he could and just be open to whatever happened. I explained that the experience almost never conforms to the experiencer's expectations and having expectations can actually inhibit the IADC.

After the first attempt at induction, Larry reported a very vague image of his father in a cloudy, heavenly place just as he had imagined it would be. As he described the scene, it was apparent that he had created the image using his imagination and the preconceptions he had about a heavenly place. He was thwarting the IADC with his expectations. I reminded him just to go with whatever happened and began another set of eye movements to induce the IADC.

This time he experienced "darkness, not scary, but a warm, friendly darkness." It was clear that an IADC was beginning to unfold. I did another set of eye movements to relax him and asked him to close his eyes again. A minute later, he opened them and said, "The veil started to lift, but not all the way. I saw my father from a distance, walking on a path with a bright blue sky in the background. I wasn't close enough to see his face."

I administered some more eye movements for relaxation and then a final set for another induction.

This time, he said his father appeared "as clearly as I am looking at you right now." He explained that his father was dressed in white with "a bright, but indistinct background." His father's face appeared very relaxed, not at all the exhausted, worn face he had when he was alive.

He told his father that he loved him, and his father said, "I know you do, and I love you too." He reported that his father also told him that he needed to pay more attention to his daughter at this time; Larry knew exactly what his father meant.

After the experience, Larry's issue of unfinished business was completely resolved. He was also amazed by his experience. He said, as many other patients have, that he never actually heard his father's voice, but that his father's words came to him in a very clear manner. He also remarked that his experience was very different from his expectation that he would see his father in a spiritual body with a heavenly background. He was surprised by the familiar, earthly appearance of the scene, although he added, "Everything I saw was very beautiful."

IADCs Have Been Experienced without Intentional Induction

The conditions necessary to have an IADC can be present without intentionally trying to induce the IADC. Before I discovered the IADC procedure and was intentionally using it with patients, 15 percent of my patients were experiencing IADCs after core-focused EMDR without my consciously helping them come to a receptive state. It appears that they were simply open and receptive after the core-focused EMDR. Other therapists who use EMDR in the standard way have also reported inadvertently inducing an IADC experience. I estimate that the percentage is much lower than the 15 percent that resulted from core-focused EMDR, however—perhaps around two percent or three percent.

The following graph shows the percentage of successful IADC inductions with three conditions:

1. Standard EMDR with no core-focused EMDR and no EMDR to enhance receptivity
2. Core-focused EMDR but no EMDR to enhance receptivity
3. Both core-focused EMDR and EMDR to enhance receptivity

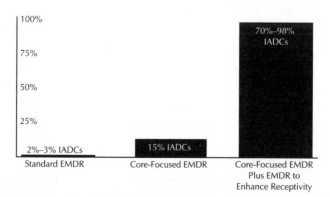

Percentage of Subjects Experiencing ADCs When Each Step Was Added

Greg's Patient's Case: "He just forgave me for abandoning him."

Greg Rimoldi described one of these surprise IADCs a patient experienced while he used core-focused EMDR. At this time, Greg had not yet begun to induce IADCs intentionally. This is Greg's report:

Two days after beginning therapy with me, the guy's older brother died. He was pretty shaken about it. I hadn't been using IADC therapy at that time, but was using core-focused EMDR. I did core-focused EMDR with him and his sadness increased a great deal.

After a final set of eye movements, he sat for a moment, eyes closed. He said he saw a bright light. I asked him what his response was to seeing it. He said, "It's gone."

I wasn't sure what to make of this, but knew that we needed to keep his focus on it. I asked him to keep an open mind. I did another set of eye movements and he closed his eyes. "I see the light again," he said with his eyes closed. "That can't be. Wait. . . . It's my brother."

"Can you talk to him?" I asked, wondering where my patient's experience would go next.

"He just went back through the light," he said and opened his eyes, crying.

"Why are you crying?" I asked.

"He just forgave me for abandoning him."

My patient explained that he thought he had no deep grief issues with the impending memorial service, but he felt great anguish when the intrusive thought kept coming to him that he had abandoned his brother. He and his older brother had some drug-use issues and would hang out together but often get into fights over drugs. Eventually, he left his brother and went to another state. Ever since, he had had nagging feelings that he had abandoned his brother. The feelings surfaced dramatically after his brother's untimely death.

It appeared that I unintentionally helped the patient enter the receptive attitude when I did the core-focused EMDR and said, "Keep an open mind."

Examples of Patients Unable to Experience an IADC

In some cases, the patient goes through a normal induction process, but the IADC does not follow.

Example 1: Miles, Who Intellectualized to Avoid Emotions

Miles was a highly avoidant individual who used intellectualization as a defense to avoid distressing emotional content. He reported traumatic memories, but typically avoided addressing them by using therapy sessions as a means to engage in abstract discourse with me. He was aware of his defense, but unable or unwilling to allow himself to engage meaningfully in the therapeutic process.

He did go along with the EMDR eye movements and several IADC induction procedures. During the IADC induction attempts, however, he would distract himself. After opening his eyes, he might remark, "I just had an insight. This is much like Zen. It provides me with an opportunity to survey the internal landscape."

"What did you find there?" I might respond, knowing it would be anything but the core emotions yet undiscovered in that wilderness.

"I find that the mind is like a cornucopia. When one thought is harvested, another fills its place to be picked and enjoyed." And on and on.

Rather than go with the experience, he found himself thinking about the situation or what the experience should be like or anything else to distract himself from whatever was buried in the hills of that internal landscape.

In the end, I resorted to a more cognitive approach to therapy that was helpful, but never did help him address the deep-seated core feelings he had.

Example 2: Phyllis, Who Was Pressured into Going into Therapy

Some of her family members pressured Phyllis into coming in for therapy, and she was very vocal about this fact in every session. "I don't know why I came today," she would say. "Can we cut this one a little short? I have lots of things to do."

During some sessions, she would make weak attempts to discuss the loss of her father, who had died six months before after years of suffering from cancer. When we went through the steps for the IADC induction, however, she would pull out and stop. She eventually confessed to me that the eye movement was bringing up memories of childhood abuse. She had not told me before this that she had been abused.

It was clear that Phyllis needed to deal with her childhood traumas before she could make progress on her more recent loss. Because of the nature of her abuse, when it became apparent that she was not going to confide in me about what happened, I suggested that perhaps a female therapist would be more to her liking. She was not interested in a referral, and soon terminated psychotherapy.

A Patient Has an IADC but Is Not Healed Because He Terminates the Process Prematurely

Bert's case is one of the very few cases in which the IADC did not result in immediate healing, probably because Bert interpreted the IADC as reinforcing his notions about the deaths and did not complete the IADC process.

During a battle in Vietnam, Bert saw two of his buddies fall some distance from him. He couldn't get to the bodies to retrieve them because the enemy was putting out too much fire. The enemy fire intensified and his unit had to pull back and leave the bodies behind. They were never retrieved.

For nearly 27 years, Bert experienced grief over the deaths of his friends and profound guilt over leaving their bodies behind.

Bert finished his story and told me he was deeply upset and felt his guilt would never go away. I administered eye movements to decrease the intensity of some of the intrusive aspects of the incident, then explained the IADC procedure to him. He expressed some reservation, but in spite of his misgivings, felt such grief and guilt that he was willing to try anything. I induced an IADC fairly rapidly.

After Bert opened his eyes, he explained to me what had happened in the IADC. He almost immediately went back to the place where the deaths had occurred 27 years earlier. In his IADC, he was closer to the two soldiers who died and could see what looked like their spirits rising out of their bodies at the moment of death. They then proceeded in a direction away from Bert.

Bert interpreted what happened as indicating his friends "left me again," upsetting him. Although some further EMDR considerably reduced his distress, he chose not to do another IADC induction because he found it to be too painful. I am convinced that had Bert chosen to continue, he would have achieved complete resolution.

13

Striking Similarities between ADCs and NDEs

Fortunately [psycho]analysis is not the only way to resolve inner conflicts. Life itself still remains a very effective therapist.

—Karen Horney

Early in the process of discovering IADCs, I realized that what my patients were describing was much like what people were reporting as near-death experiences (NDEs) and after-death communications (ADCs).

People position themselves into two sharply divided camps on NDE and ADC phenomena: the afterlife believers and the afterlife skeptics. Unfortunately, the entrenched positions each camp has taken have limited exploration of the effects of NDEs and ADCs apart from discussions of personal beliefs.

An NDE is an experience a person has while clinically dead or near death. The person is then revived and lives to tell what he or she experienced when closest to death. Recent scientific evidence has indicated that these experiences often occur when there is no brain function. Those who study NDEs describe some common themes:

- Out-of-body experience
- Meeting deceased friends and relatives
- Feeling of peacefulness and well-being
- Going through a tunnel toward light
- Beautiful landscapes
- Life review

ADCs are experiences in which people believe they have communicated with someone after the person's death. In *Hello from Heaven!*, Bill and Judy Guggenheim list the 12 most frequent types of after-death communication people report having with their deceased loved ones:

1. *Sentient ADCs* are one of the most common types and involve sensing or feeling the presence of the deceased, described as "the least tangible and most subtle form of ADC contact."

2. *Auditory ADCs* are also common and involve hearing the voice of the deceased or receiving a verbal message.

3. *Tactile ADCs* involve feeling a physical touch from the deceased and are relatively less common.

4. *Olfactory ADCs,* which are relatively common, involve smelling a fragrance that is associated with the deceased.

5. *Visual ADCs* involve seeing the deceased, and are both common and relatively dramatic compared to other forms of ADCs.

6. *ADC visions* are experienced either with eyes open or closed, and may include some form of two-way communication. These visions are distinguished from visual ADCs by the "bright, vivid colors that radiate their own inner light." This type of ADC is less common.

7. *Twilight ADCs* occur just as people are falling asleep or waking up. Any combination of the above ADCs can be involved in this form of ADC. These experiences are fairly common.

8. *Sleep state ADCs* are very common and occur when a person is asleep, but are experienced as very different from dreams. Like twilight ADCs, sleep state ADCs can take on a variety of forms.

9. *Out-of-body or OBE ADCs* are less common and involve contact with the deceased while the survivor is in an out-of-body state. Some of these ADCs are very NDE-like and include going through a tunnel toward light before meeting the deceased.

10. *Telephone ADCs* take place either when a person is awake or asleep. When asleep, it is similar to a sleep state ADC. Some people, however, have actually reported receiving a phone call from the deceased while awake. This is the least common form of ADC.

11. *ADCs of physical phenomena* are rather common and involve unusual physical events that survivors perceive as a message from the deceased. Examples include a light being turned on or off or a door being opened or closed.

12. *Symbolic ADCs* are common and involve seeing something in the physical environment that survivors interpret as a sign from the deceased, such as butterflies, rainbows, and so on.

NDEs and ADCs and their similarities to IADCs are explained in the pages that follow.

Near-Death Experiences (NDEs)

When I first read Dr. Raymond Moody's *Life after Life* many years ago, I was very skeptical that an NDE was anything more than some sort of a psychological or physiologically based hallucination that occurred infrequently. Dr. Moody made the point, however, that people who have NDEs generally do not share their experience with others because they learn rather quickly that people tend to dismiss their experiences as symptoms of temporary insanity. He explained that they share their experiences only when asked.

So I began to ask. I not only discovered that the experience is common, but those who have had the experience are absolutely convinced it was a real event. It is also very common for those who have had NDEs to no longer fear death.

Since then, I have had the opportunity to talk to a few hundred people who have experienced NDEs. Most of these reports were provided by people who were normal, psychologically healthy individuals. The NDEs were often life changing for those who experienced them.

One patient named Pete had both an NDE and an IADC experience. He described them as having the same quality and psychological impact.

Pete's Case: "I saw and talked to the guys in my squad, all six of them."

Pete had grown very close to his fellow squad members over the months they spent together in Vietnam. "We loved each other more than family," he said to me in my office. One day, the North Vietnamese launched a major attack and infiltrated their base camp, throwing explosives everywhere and shooting as many Americans as they could. All the members of Pete's squad were either killed immediately or mortally wounded, except Pete who was uninjured. As the enemy continued to kill Americans all around him, Pete pulled his six comrades' bodies one by one into a bunker. One of his friends had been decapitated by an explosion and another bled to death in his arms. All were dead by the time help arrived.

Although Pete was awarded a medal for his actions, the event was his psychological undoing. An Army psychiatrist incorrectly diagnosed him as a paranoid schizophrenic and sent him back to the States. For the next 30 years, he suffered from frequent, severe intrusive thoughts and nightmares of the incident.

Over several psychotherapy sessions with me, Pete began to access the memories tormenting him, but which he had not faced since the time of the incident. When he began reliving the memories for the first time, he came to the verge of losing control, sobbing with his face in his hands.

I began EMDR immediately to decrease the intensity of his traumatic images and feelings. It reduced the distress to a manageable degree, and he then agreed to an IADC induction. I performed the IADC procedure three times and the IADC began on the third try. He closed his eyes, thinking of the soldier who had died in his arms. He continued to cry for a few seconds, but then the tears abruptly stopped and he began to smile. He continued to smile with his eyes closed for two or three minutes. He then opened his eyes, beaming.

"I saw and talked to the guys in my squad, all six of them. They all looked happy, healthy, and at peace. I told them I had been waiting for this day for a long time, and I heard them say, 'So have we.'"

Pete then described how they exchanged expressions of affection for each other. "I heard one of them say, just as clearly as I can hear you, 'We'll all be here for you when it is your time.'"

All of Pete's issues related to the loss of his squad were completely resolved on that day. Toward the end of the session, he said he had experienced a near-death experience (NDE) during a serious childhood illness and that people in both his NDE and this IADC had a similar appearance and communicated in the same telepathic, emotionally powerful way. Pete said his NDE and IADC had similar effects on him, and he believed the two were the same kind of experience.

For the next three weeks of psychotherapy, Pete spent much of his time talking about the fond memories he had of his squad, memories he had not been able to think of before because they caused such distress. I saw Pete again eight months after he was discharged from the hospital. He reported that he no longer suffered from intrusive memories of the incident and he continued to have only good feelings about his fellow squad members.

Similarities between the NDE and IADC Experiences

We have observed remarkable similarities between NDEs and IADCs in the following areas:

- Out-of-body experience
- Seeing the deceased as whole, functioning, and healthy
- Feeling of peacefulness and well-being
- Going through a tunnel toward light
- Meeting the deceased
- Beautiful landscapes
- Life review
- Some deceased are in bright light, others in dim areas
- Shared experiences

A summary of the similarities in each of these areas follows.

Out-of-Body Experience

People who have an NDE (NDErs) frequently report an out-of-body experience, usually floating above their physical bodies watching medical technicians try to revive them. IADC experiencers do not report out-of-body experiences, but they frequently report going back to the scene of the death of the person for whom they are grieving and witnessing the spirit moving out of the body. These experiences occur most frequently when there was no personal relationship between the survivor and the deceased, such as cases reported by a health care provider in a hospital or a soldier witnessing a battlefield death.

Bob's Case: He saw what looked like the spirits of the woman and child rise out of their bodies at the moment they died.

Bob and his unit had set up camp for the night in Vietnam. He and his two buddies had guard duty and were ordered to shoot anything that moved outside their perimeter. Later that night, they detected movement in the bush not far from their position. All three opened fire, and it appeared that they hit whoever or whatever it was. For their safety, they had to wait for daylight to go out and see what it was.

That morning, they all went out and discovered that they had shot and killed a Vietnamese woman and her infant. The woman was unarmed and for some unknown reason had wandered close to their camp. At the time, Bob was enraged at the senselessness of what had happened. In the many years since the incident, Bob had suffered from daily intrusive images of their dead bodies and intense feelings of anger and sadness.

When Bob explained his memory in our psychotherapy session, his primary feeling was overwhelming sadness. The second time I performed the IADC procedure, he closed his eyes and spontaneously went back to the moment that the mother and child were killed. Although he didn't see the bodies until the next morning, in his IADC he saw what looked like the spirits of the woman and child rise out of their bodies at the moment they died. The mother held her child in her arms and drifted through a large tunnel toward a bright light. He reported that they had a very peaceful look on their faces and appeared to move toward the light with a sense of purpose.

Bob opened his eyes and told me about his experience. "I feel like my sadness has been replaced by real happiness." He was greatly comforted by his perception that life continued for the mother and child, as well as by his feeling that the mother and child had maintained their loving relationship. He believed that his experience proved that there is a life after death.

Bob was somewhat confused, however, by the appearance of the bright light during his IADC, because at the time of the incident, it was totally dark. Bob was unaware of NDEs and knew nothing of the consistent theme of a tunnel and bright light in NDE accounts. The report came solely from what he perceived during his IADC.

A month later, after Bob had successfully worked through another issue, he ended his psychotherapy. At that time, he no longer felt any sadness or anger about this incident, and all associated negative images had disappeared.

Seeing the Deceased as Whole, Functioning, and Healthy

When NDErs report meeting loved ones who have passed away, they describe them as being whole and healthy, even if they were disabled in life. The same is true of descriptions of the deceased in IADCs. All physical impairments or imperfections are reported as being gone. People who were very old or ill before death are always experienced as younger and healthier. Children who die very young are frequently experienced as older. A face that was worry-worn in life always looks peaceful and serene.

Mary's Case: Her sister no longer had the physical deformities and her mental abilities seemed much more advanced than they had been.

Mary's family moved frequently when she was a child, so it was difficult for her to develop friendships. Her only sibling was her older sister, who had been seriously disabled from birth. Her sister's mental age never exceeded five years old. Mary provided much of the daily caretaking for her sister, but she never considered her sister to be a burden because she was a companion when Mary had no friends. She felt fortunate to have a sister whom she loved dearly and thought of as her best friend. Mary described her sister as fun-loving and always happy.

When Mary was 14, her sister's health declined and her seizures became more frequent. One evening, when their parents were out, her sister had an unusually severe seizure and died in Mary's arms.

Mary didn't talk or eat for days and for the next year experienced problems at school. Over the years, however, Mary managed to grieve her loss and went on to live a fulfilling life with her own large family and professional success. When she discussed her sister's death in my office, she did so with only residual, normal sadness.

I talked with Mary about the IADC procedure, telling her some people experience a reconnection with the deceased loved one. She was an atheist, she said, and had a disdain for all religious practices. She agreed to attempt the induction, but only out of an intellectual curiosity.

In spite of her reluctance, the IADC began almost immediately after the core-focused EMDR had uncovered her sadness and started to bring it down. In her IADC, Mary first experienced "a brilliant white light." Then her sister came out of the light and said, "I love you, Mary." Mary then felt that she somehow mentally said back to her, "I love you too."

Her sister told her that all the pain Mary suffered after her death was unnecessary. Her sister no longer had the physical deformities she had when alive, and Mary noted later that her mental abilities seemed much more advanced than they had been. Mary reported that her sister then retreated back into the light and was gone.

After her IADC, Mary was ecstatic. She was completely convinced that she had seen and spoken with her sister. Mary felt reconnected to her sister and joyous about her sister's well-being, with no residual sadness.

Feeling of Peacefulness and Well-Being

Most of those who have had NDEs report peacefulness and well-being for themselves. IADC experiencers report the deceased as feeling peaceful and happy, a feeling that somehow is transmitted from the deceased to them. For the IADC patient, experiencing the deceased to be in such a profoundly positive emotional state does much to expedite the resolution of grief.

Going through a Tunnel toward Light

People who experience NDEs sometimes experience traveling through a tunnel or passageway. In the same way, people experiencing IADCs sometimes feel as though they go through a tunnel or passageway before meeting the deceased. NDEs and IADCs also share the description of a bright light at the end of the tunnel. People who experience IADCs somehow know that the deceased is in the light at the end of the tunnel and are either moving through it with a sense of purpose or being drawn toward it.

Meeting the Deceased

People who have had NDEs often describe meeting or sensing the presence of people significant to them who are deceased, usually family members or close friends. In the same way, IADCs always involve people of importance to the experiencer, although in IADCs, the deceased may have become significant through a brief, dramatic encounter, such as being killed by the experiencer in battle. The loving feelings from the deceased in NDEs are the same as those the IADC experiencers feel during their sessions.

Beautiful Landscapes

Beautiful landscapes are very common in NDEs and IADCs, with picturesque trees, green hills, flowering bushes, lush expanses of grass, shimmering lakes, and streams. Colors are typically brighter and richer, sometimes described as radiant or iridescent. Both NDE and IADC experiencers say the environment exudes a feeling of peace and serenity that is transmitted to the experiencer. Sometimes people with expectations based on their religious beliefs are surprised by the familiar but richer earthly environments in their IADC experiences.

Life Review

In the life review portion of the NDE, the person who is near death may experience his or her entire life or key moments in a very brief period of time. The life review typically includes a special focus on the feelings the person experienced during specific incidents, as well as the positive or negative feelings the others involved felt as a result of the person's actions. Those who have life reviews as part of their NDEs report that they are profound, life-changing learning experiences. They frequently develop increased empathy and an interest in helping others as a result of them.

IADC experiencers do not experience their own life review or any portion of the deceased's life review. The deceased, however, are consistently described as appearing as though they had been through a life review and as having learned from their mistakes, taken responsibility for their actions, and become very interested in correcting whatever suffering or pain they caused other people during life.

Some Deceased Are in Bright Light, Others in Dim Areas

Dr. Raymond Moody wrote in *Reflections on Life after Life* that NDErs often report the deceased being in brightly lit surroundings or exuding bright light. They also report a counterpart "realm of bewildered spirits" that is dimly lit or dulled. The experiencers report that the people in the dimly lit area are there to solve problems that are keeping them from moving toward the light.

This description is consistent with the reports by IADC experiencers that most of their deceased loved ones are in bright light or exude bright light. Deceased who have lived troubled lives and have done great harm to others, however, are consistently described as being in a dimly lit or gray area, being remorseful, and wanting to alleviate the problems they left behind.

Shared Experiences

In *The Last Laugh,* Dr. Moody mentions the concept of the "shared near-death experience" or "empathic near-death experience" in which someone with a person who is dying shares what seems to be the dying person's near-death experience: feeling the sense of going through a tunnel toward a beautiful light and perceiving deceased relatives coming to greet the dying person.

This unusual experience parallels the "shared IADCs" that observers and therapists have experienced while the patient is having an IADC (see chapter 8).

Comparison of the Quality of the NDEs and IADC Experiences

All of our patients who have had both an NDE and an IADC are convinced that the two experiences are essentially the same phenomenon experienced from different points of view. In every case, they report that the two experiences have the same qualities and psychological impact. These patients also believe with great certainty that their NDEs and IADC experiences have tapped into the same source.

Nancy's experience provides a clear example of the close relationship between the two experiences.

Nancy's Case: Her IADC was "much clearer and more focused" than her NDE.

Nancy's pregnancy was uneventful until the ninth month when she began vomiting and could no longer feel her baby's movement. An ultrasound revealed no fetal heartbeat, so labor was induced and her baby was delivered dead. During the induced labor, Nancy went into hypertensive shock and remained near death for three days. At some time during those three days, Nancy experienced an NDE in which she saw her mother, who had died a few years earlier, holding her baby. They seemed very happy. Her baby was looking up at his grandmother. Nancy told me that her mother said to her, "It's OK." Behind them, Nancy saw "a bright comforting light."

These events happened six years prior to our therapy session. In spite of her NDE, she continued to experience grief over her baby's death, especially around the day that would have been her baby's birthday.

After she explained what had happened, I described IADCs. Nancy was enthusiastic about the IADC procedure because her NDE had convinced her that such experiences were possible. After the IADC induction, Nancy closed her eyes. Very quickly, she reported that she again saw her son with her mother and they both looked happy and peaceful. There were notable differences between her NDE and her IADC experience, however. She said her son looked older and much healthier than he did before, and instead of looking at his grandmother, he was looking at Nancy and reaching out with both hands toward her.

In the NDE, Nancy felt that her mother and infant son were moving away from her, but she had the clear sense that they were moving toward her in the IADC. There was also no bright light behind them in the IADC as there had been in her NDE. After her IADC, Nancy explained that her IADC was "much clearer and more focused" than her NDE. She experienced her IADC as more comforting because of her sense that her mother and son were moving toward her, not away.

At the end of the session, Nancy said she felt a much stronger connection with both her son and mother, and she believed her grief had fully resolved. Seven months later, in a follow-up session, she said her grief was still fully resolved. She was convinced that her IADC was not merely the memory of her NDE, that they were two separate experiences tapping into the same source.

The remarkable similarities between NDEs and IADCs suggest that they are closely related phenomena, likely from the same source. The fact that we can now reliably induce these experiences in a controlled laboratory setting provides us, for the first time, with a means to evaluate them in an objective and scientific way. A number of different competing beliefs and theories can now be put to a more rigorous test, and perhaps we can understand the source and nature of these phenomena.

Spontaneous ADCs

I named the procedure that results in an experience of an after-death communication an induced after-death communication (IADC) after reading Bill and Judy Guggenheim's best-selling *Hello from Heaven!* Most remarkable to me is that the 353 personal accounts of spontaneous ADCs in their book are nearly identical to the descriptions my patients have been reporting. My patients also volunteer accounts of their spontaneous ADCs that all contain the same characteristics as the reports of IADCs.

Dave's Case: "She reached out for me and gave me a hug and a kiss."

Dave was an adult patient of mine working on a problem other than grief over his mother's death, but the issue of her death surfaced. He had no grief at all about it because it had happened when he was five years old and he had a spontaneous ADC when he was six that eliminated the grief.

Dave was an only child and his father had left the family a few years before his mother's death. He was alone with his mother when she collapsed and died of a heart attack.

An aunt came by two hours later and found Dave sitting by his mother's body, crying. For the next several months, Dave lived with the same aunt, but he interacted only minimally with other people and felt extremely alone. He was disturbed by frequent and intrusive images and thoughts of his mother's death, especially in nightmares.

For a year after her death, he had a recurring dream in which he was traveling through a tunnel toward a light he could see in the distance, but he always awoke before getting to the end of the tunnel. One night, however, he reached the end of the tunnel and his mother was there, standing with a bright shining light behind her.

"She looked very peaceful and happy," he recalled, "and she said she was all right and that she would always be with me. I can remember very clearly that she reached out for me and gave me a hug and a kiss."

Although Dave didn't know what to make of the experience at age six, it completely changed him. From that point on, he was no longer bothered by intrusive symptoms and no longer felt alone. He also began to interact with others in a normal, healthy way. He could distinctly recall a time in the days after the ADC when he was walking down the street feeling good about his mother. Although Dave's ADC had occurred many years in the past, he continued to feel at peace with his mother's death.

Dave's case illustrates that, even for a child, the spontaneous ADC is a positive experience that can heal grief, just as an IADC does.

Differences between Spontaneous ADCs and IADCs

The most prominent difference between spontaneous ADCs and IADCs is that in spontaneous ADCs, the experience occurs randomly and unexpectedly; the experiencer does not anticipate having the experience. In an IADC, a psychotherapist helps the experiencer enter a receptive mode that allows the IADC to occur. The psychotherapist does not create the IADC or even influence its direction. The role of the psychotherapist is simply to aid the experiencer to come to an open, receptive state so the IADC can occur on its own. From that point on, the content is generally unexpected, just as the content of a spontaneous ADC is.

There are the three important differences between spontaneous ADCs and IADCs:

1. The Guggenheims and others who have written books on spontaneous ADCs state that they always occur without warning and cannot be induced. We have proven that the psychological state necessary for the experience to occur can be induced, although the ADC itself unfolds naturally, without interference, after the receptive state has been induced.

2. IADCs tend to be more elaborate, richer in content, and more multisensory than most spontaneous ADCs. IADCs are never inferred or vague, as are sentient, physical, and symbolic ADCs, and most involve a combination of the sensory experiences present in visual, auditory, and tactile ADCs.

3. IADCs not only accelerate the grieving process, as spontaneous ADCs do, but in nearly all cases, the more extensive, controlled nature of the induced experience completely resolves the grief, a result much stronger than the effects of most spontaneous ADCs. If all issues are not resolved with an IADC, it is a rather simple matter to immediately induce the experience again while having the patient attend to what is not yet resolved. Any additional, leftover issue rapidly resolves with the next induction. The procedure can easily be repeated until all issues are fully resolved.

For example, in an IADC already presented in this book, Gary had established a connection with his deceased daughter in an IADC, but still felt some sadness because he missed her. I asked him to hold that concern in mind and began another IADC. This time, his daughter told him, "I'm still with you, Daddy." His sadness completely resolved. It is clear that if he had experienced only the first part of his ADC in a spontaneous ADC and had no way to continue the experience, he would have been left with some sadness.

Some IADC Experiencers Have Had or Then Have Spontaneous ADCs

People who have had both spontaneous ADCs and IADCs report, without exception, that both of the experiences have the same quality and impact on the experiencer. In some cases, the less direct, spontaneous ADC experiences have provided a starting point from which more elaborate IADC experiences have developed.

Some of our patients' experiences of spontaneous ADCs have been very rich in content and very similar to IADCs. The following case provides a good example of a rather elaborate spontaneous ADC reported to me by a patient.

Jerry's Case: "Nobody can ever tell me that it wasn't real, not you or anyone else."

Jerry had come to see me for psychotherapy about an unrelated matter, but after developing some trust in me, felt he could tell me his spontaneous ADC story "without being labeled a nutcase." Jerry was living in the Midwest and his ex-wife was living on the East Coast with their three children. One night, he experienced the clear image of his ex-wife while he was asleep.

"She looked beautiful, peaceful, and happy," he said, "and she wanted to tell me about something of great concern to her." Jerry said she told him that he needed to start playing a more important role in rearing their children and even offered very specific suggestions about each child. Jerry said his experience was much clearer than a dream.

Jerry awoke right after his experience, baffled by its remarkable clarity. He could remember the entire experience, and for him it felt like a real conversation with his ex-wife. After lying awake for a while trying to make sense of his experience, he managed to get back to sleep.

The next morning as he was making coffee, the phone rang. It was his ex-wife's sister. Tearfully, she told Jerry that his ex-wife had been killed in a car accident during the night.

Suddenly, the meaning of his experience became clear. Since then, Jerry's ex-wife has appeared to him five times in spontaneous ADCs, each time offering further advice about their children. "Every time," he said, "she did all the talking." And after each experience, Jerry followed her advice closely. In all instances, the advice turned out to be very helpful.

As he told me the story, Jerry laughed at one point and said, "She hasn't changed much. She was always hyperverbal and bossy." When I asked him if he thought that his wife had really visited him after she died, he said defiantly, "I am sure of it. I am as sure of it as I am that I'm looking at you right now. Nobody can ever tell me that it wasn't real, not you or anyone else. I don't care what other people think about this because they really don't know. I didn't believe in this stuff before it happened, but now I have no doubt whatsoever."

Jerry's description of his experience had the identical tone that my patients have when they describe IADCs. His ADC and my patients' IADCs were both remarkably clear and resulted in dramatic resolution of grief.

It is apparent that IADCs and spontaneous ADCs are essentially identical, with the only difference being that the psychological state necessary to have the IADC experience can be purposefully induced by a psychotherapist.

14

The Good News: You Can
Now Take a Look for Yourself

Doubt is not a pleasant condition, but certainty is absurd.

—Voltaire

Primary Conclusions about IADC Therapy

After years of successful IADCs with thousands of patients by a growing number of psychotherapists, we have come to three conclusions:

1. We can very rapidly, reliably, and easily induce an IADC in a high percentage of people interested in having the experience.

2. The IADCs I and my colleagues induce heal the most painful, primary,
core elements of grief: the deep, profound sadness and associated sense
of disconnection.

3. Many of my patients report the same experiences described by people
who have had a near-death experience (NDE) or spontaneous after-
death communication (ADC).

The Source of the Phenomenon, for Now, Is Irrelevant

Some therapists will insist on knowing the source of the IADC phenomenon before they begin to use it in their therapy or, more pointedly, they will say, "We can't have voodoo science mixed in with serious therapy." I agree. But I'm asserting that the origin of the experience doesn't make any difference when considering it as a means of healing our patients.

We do not insist on knowing the gene that results in a thumb to teach someone how to hold a hammer. A thumb is simply a tool in every human being's repertoire. We teach people to grasp hammers with their thumbs and fingers without regard for where their thumbs come from. So it must be with IADC therapy, at least for now.

Occasionally, as you consider IADC therapy, you will stop for a moment and your mind will drift into eddies of thought about this strange phenomenon. It is remarkable and powerful. You will often, as I have, speculate on its origins. This appears inevitable. However, we have attempted not to steer you toward one belief or another.

For now at least, it doesn't matter what I believe or what the other psychotherapists using IADC therapy believe. No one asks whether the professional explaining a psychoanalytic or behavioral therapy method is a Christian, agnostic, Jew, Muslim, or Buddhist before deciding to use the methods the speaker describes. Their beliefs are irrelevant. We look at the results of the methods and apply them as they are appropriate and efficacious for our patients. Of course, all of us have some beliefs about agency in the universe and the afterlife, even if we are agnostics. But no two of us using IADC therapy have the same beliefs. Our beliefs are simply irrelevant to its use.

Value of IADCs to Therapy

IADC therapy should become a common tool in the psychologist's repertoire. Clinical experience based on thousands of cases at this point demonstrates that the procedure simply works.

It appears that the ADC, IADC, and NDE phenomena are natural, normal parts of the human organism. Like an inoculation's effect on the immune system, IADC therapy stimulates the patients' abilities to heal themselves. The IADC procedure enables patients to access this healing capability and allow it to do the healing with little intervention from the therapist and no conscious effort by the patient at the moment the experience unfolds.

A materialist social scientist might retort, "But it's based on delusion. Dead people can't talk." Well, the fact is that if we insisted that patients' thinking conform to our conception of what is rational and logical, we would do precious little therapy. The mental constructs on which a person has built a functioning, healthy psyche are idiosyncratic, irrational, and value-laden. We help the patient integrate these constructs into socially acceptable thought and behavior that work for the patient and promise future psychological health. Whether they are all true and logical is incidental to mental health.

IADC therapy works. It heals patients. It provides an inner confidence and strength that sustains the healing. What more can we ask?

If research supports these clinical findings, I believe it would be unethical for a psychotherapist not to use IADC therapy with people who grieve.

Look through the Telescope

In 1513, Nicolaus Copernicus concluded from his observations that the sun is at the center of our solar system. He was ridiculed by most of his contemporary scientists and philosophers. Nearly a hundred years later, in 1609, Galileo asked scientists of the time to look through a telescope so they could see for themselves that Copernicus was right. But his adversaries were so sure he was wrong that they refused even to look. The fact that the sun is the center of the solar system wasn't fully accepted until decades later.

We are suggesting that, regardless of your belief system, just take a look. IADCs can be induced at will, so anyone can explore the phenomena apparent in ADCs and NDEs by having a qualified therapist induce an IADC. The only informed opinion regarding the ultimate nature of the experience is one that comes from someone who has had the experience.

Although an overwhelming majority of the IADC experiencers are convinced of the spiritual authenticity of the experience, for now it doesn't matter what you believe, what we believe, or even what the experiencers believe. The IADC experience heals grief and trauma in a very short time and appears to be sustained long-term. The technique has worth because it works; it doesn't require us to agree on a belief system or theory about the source of the phenomenon to support it.

One conclusion is clear: The IADC procedure described in this book offers the means to alleviate a great amount of human suffering. There is no more debilitating pain in life than losing a child, a battlefield buddy, or a spouse of many years and feeling disconnected forever. We lose a part of ourselves when someone so important to us disappears from existence. Now, we can routinely heal this deep pain as well as the anger and guilt that sometimes accompany it.

IADC therapy is unusual and will continue to be controversial until it becomes a commonly used method of therapy. Anyone who wishes to verify its efficacy, however, can explore the method and its effects at will just by engaging in a session with a qualified therapist and experiencing an IADC firsthand. I invite any psychologist, social worker, psychiatrist, or other professional in the healing community to experience the IADC phenomenon. Judge for yourself. Just look through the telescope.

15

The Future of IADC Therapy—
Where Do We Go from Here?

There are two ways to slide easily through life: to believe everything or to doubt everything; both ways save us from thinking.
—Alfred Korzybski (founder of the general semantics movement)

Research into IADCs, ADCs, and NDEs

So far, we have only clinical observation data about IADCs and their
effects on grief. Controlled studies must be performed in which the IADC
treatment and outcomes are investigated to help us understand these
remarkable events. Researchers at the University of North Texas, under
the direction of Janice Holden, Ed.D., are preparing to complete such
research. They also plan formal study of shared IADCs in scientifically controlled settings. Their findings should be available sometime after publication of this book. I hope that other university departments will become
involved in the near future.

IADC therapy also provides researchers with a psychological event sufficiently similar to NDEs and spontaneous ADCs to study the nature of all

of these phenomena so inferences can be made about them. It is to be hoped that neuroimaging studies will be conducted to help us understand the activities in the brain that are related to these experiences. Of course, even if we are able to identify the areas of the brain that are active during an IADC experience, that doesn't necessarily mean that the experience has its genesis there. For example, knowing that the occipital lobes of my brain become activated when I look at a tree certainly does not mean that I am hallucinating a tree. It also doesn't explain how it is that my brain activity gives rise to my subjective experience of the tree.

David Chalmers, Ph.D., a well-known and respected leader in the field of the philosophy of consciousness, has argued that relating brain mechanisms to conscious experience is the "easy" problem in the study of consciousness. The "hard" problem is in understanding how or why physical processes in our brains give rise to our subjective experiences. Dr. Chalmers points out that the reductive approaches taken in solving the easy problems fail to explain the hard problems.

All of our work has been with adults. Since children both experience spontaneous ADCs and respond well to EMDR, however, I suspect that IADCs would work well with children. The only limiting factors may be the child's ability (depending on age) or willingness to tolerate core-focused EMDR. IADC therapy should be considered for use with children, and its effects on young people in grief should be studied.

Receiving Training

We are training psychotherapists to induce IADCs. For information about training, go to the Web site at http://induced-adc.com, or call Dr. Botkin at the Center for Grief and Traumatic Loss, LLC in Libertyville, Illinois (847-680-0279).

Making Appointments with Therapists in Your Area

You can learn about trained therapists in your area by going to the Web site at http://induced-adc.com.

Central Clearinghouse for Research

The authors provide a clearinghouse for research into the IADC phe-nomenon at http://induced-adc.com. We invite researchers and those interested in reading the research to log on to the Web site to learn more about the research being done and contribute to the body of knowledge that will grow as more therapists learn to perform IADCs.

16

A Personal Statement

Initially, ADCs occurred by accident with patients I was treating for grief and traumatic loss. Not only did I not anticipate my patients' experiences, but after they occurred, I had no idea what they were. The only thing clear to me was these experiences healed my patients to a degree I hadn't thought possible. I found myself hesitant to share this discovery because I knew full well the likely reaction from colleagues, all of whom had been trained to exercise a healthy degree of skepticism. I wouldn't have believed it myself.

I am well aware that I am going to antagonize many people entrenched in a broad range of antithetical belief systems. Given the healing power of these experiences, however, I have come to believe I have a moral duty to share this discovery in the best way I can. Many suffering people will greatly benefit from the IADC procedure.

People often ask what my personal beliefs are. Since my primary goal is to help as many suffering people as I can, I'm hesitant to share my beliefs because they're not at all relevant to the therapeutic benefits of the procedure. IADC therapy heals grieving survivors without requiring a particular belief system. It doesn't matter what IADC experiencers believe or what the IADC therapist believes. I have trained a few therapists who regularly perform IADC therapy, but remain either agnostic or skeptical about the spiritual nature of the IADC. Nevertheless, all of their patients benefit from the experience as fully as the patients of therapists who attach spiritual significance to it. They do IADC therapy simply because it works.

When pinned down about my personal beliefs, I offer the following. IADCs must either be spiritual experiences or subjective hallucinations generated solely by our mind/brain or inner representation of the deceased that have no relationship to any world that exists separate from us. I believe that if there is an afterlife, then IADCs are true spiritual experiences. I cannot imagine that if the afterlife is a reality, IADCs, ADCs, and NDEs are hallucinatory aberrations produced by our brains that lead us into misunderstanding.

Einstein once remarked, "Subtle is the Lord, malicious He is not." He meant that while the laws of our universe are often very difficult to discern, our universe does not intend to mislead those who try to understand it. If there is no afterlife, which would mean that IADCs are pure hallucination, then perhaps our brains did evolve a hidden healing savant that reveals itself at times of great personal need such as when we approach death or suffer the death of a loved one. If the healing savant exists, then all of us have the same hidden capacity to heal.

The fact that we could tap into that capacity, study it, and use it to heal those who suffer so profoundly still constitutes a major breakthrough. I believe, therefore, that we enter a win-win position by simply using the therapy.

When humans evolved the ability to understand the world, they assigned supernatural causes to events they did not understand. Many still do that. I believe that all events will eventually be understood to result from natural law or causes. For me, this way of thinking does not diminish the magnificence of our universe and personal lives, and it does not remove God, or a Higher Power, as an initial creator of natural law. An e-mail from a listener to a radio show on which I was interviewed expressed dissatisfaction with me because I don't believe in miracles. My response to him was that I believe that everything in our universe is a miracle. I believe, therefore, that if there is an afterlife and, therefore, IADCs are real spiritual events, then they are a product of a natural law that we do not yet understand. Perhaps we are now getting closer to an understanding.

In addition to the study of IADCs, spontaneous ADCs, and NDEs, the field of biophysics has made recent advances that I believe offer a promising lead. I refer the reader to the German biophysicist Fritz Albert Popp, and to researchers around the world who study photon emission from biological systems (PEBS). This information is available on the Internet. Although these scientists are researchers and make no claims that their findings might eventually explain soul or spirit, the implications of their research should be clear to the interested reader who has some background in physics.

My life for the last ten years has been emotionally and intellectually exciting. The emotional gratification that I experience each time a patient is healed by an IADC is difficult to put into words. Other IADC therapists I have trained know that feeling well. IADCs make each session an awe-inspiring adventure. When I tell people I am a psychologist specializing in grief and trauma, they generally imagine that my work is painful and grueling. They don't know that I leave most sessions feeling upbeat and energized. It's difficult to tell people that without telling them the whole story.

The intellectual aspects of this adventure, although exciting, are somewhat more complicated. There was certainly a degree of exhilaration with each intellectual step along the way. At the same time, however, it's not easy to discard one's cherished beliefs and theories in light of mounting evidence against them. Since my primary ethical and moral duty has always been to help my patients in the best way I can, I had to abandon ways of thinking that were much more comfortable for me. A significant amount of anxiety was associated with each intellectual shift I made in the course of the IADC discovery. My own fear has been the most difficult part of this journey. I am fully aware of the risks involved, and that I will likely be attacked from a number of sides. There is certainly a part of me that doesn't want this job. The other part of me, however, is going ahead, with the hope that I can make a difference.

17

An Important Note on Suicide

Some people familiar with my work have warned me that the information presented in this book may lead some individuals to commit suicide. The reason for this concern is that in IADC therapy the deceased are consistently experienced as happy and in a better place. People who live troubled and painful lives, therefore, might see suicide as a way to get out of their difficulties and into a happier, better place. To those individuals who may consider suicide as an option, I want to offer some very clear warnings.

First, although the information provided in this book is very suggestive, it does not in any way constitute proof of an afterlife. If it is later determined that IADCs are nothing more than brain-based hallucinations, then the idea that one can commit suicide to get to a better place would be based on a potentially very costly and ultimately very mistaken interpretation of this information.

Second, even if IADCs are true glimpses into the afterlife, the idea of committing suicide to get there also comes with a very severe warning. Perhaps the most frequent message in IADC experiences is that no one "gets away" with anything, and that the suffering we cause in other people must at some point be addressed. If IADCs are real spiritual events, then people who commit suicide are not only still left with the same interpersonal issues they were trying to avoid, they also have to confront the additional issue of the pain that their suicide caused in others. It has also been reported that people who attempt suicide have a higher frequency of frightening or otherwise negative near-death experiences (NDEs).

People who experience IADCs, like those who experience NDEs, uniformly develop a markedly increased interest in living. After performing a few thousand IADCs, and some with patients who had multiple and serious prior suicide attempts, never has a patient developed an increased interest in suicide. In fact, a number of my patients, even some who lived with extreme emotional pain daily, told me sometime after their IADC experience that they no longer considered suicide as an option.

Appendix A

Glossary

ADC: After-death communication. An ADC is any experience a person has that the person describes as contact with a deceased person. ADCs are universally recognized as very healing experiences. Since they happen spontaneously, we often refer to them in this book as "spontaneous ADCs."

Core-focused EMDR: A variation of EMDR therapy originated by Dr. Allan Botkin. In core-focused EMDR, the therapist uses EMDR to directly access and process the sadness that is at the core of grief.

EMDR: Eye movement desensitization and reprocessing. A psychotherapy method developed in the 1980s by psychologist Francine Shapiro, Ph.D. The EMDR therapist guides the patient in moving his or her eyes in a particular rhythmic fashion while, at the same time, attending to a distressing thought, feeling, image, or sensation. It is believed that the movement of the eyes accelerates information processing in the brain.

Grief: Grief, as the term is used in this book, is a very individual, natural, spontaneous response to the death of another person. It is not a single emotion, however. Grief includes a wide range of emotions, especially feelings of shock, numbing, sadness, guilt, and anger.

IADC: Induced after-death communication or induced ADC. A psychotherapist follows the IADC procedure to bring the patient to a psychological state in which the patient is likely to experience an after-death communication.

NDE: Near-death experience. An NDE is an experience that takes place when a person comes close to death. Each NDE is unique to the person having it, but many similarities among NDEs have become apparent. They include:

- A sense of being outside one's body
- Moving through a tunnel or passageway toward light
- Feeling an overwhelming sense of peace
- Meeting deceased loved ones and friends
- Experiencing a life review
- Seeing beautiful or radiant landscapes
- Returning to one's body

Post-traumatic stress disorder (PTSD): PTSD develops when the person experiences an event with one or more of the following characteristics affecting the person directly or others with the person as the event occurred:

1. Someone died or someone's life was threatened.
2. Someone suffered physical injury.
3. Someone's physical integrity was violated, as in rape.

The person experiencing PTSD may have any combination of the following symptoms:

1. Reexperiencing the traumatic event through intrusive negative memories, nightmares, and flashbacks in which the person relives the event.
2. Persistent avoidance of reminders of the incident.
3. Persistent feelings of increased psychological arousal, such as fear, anxiety, or depression.

NOTE: Similarities between PTSD and grief: Grief and PTSD are similar in some important ways. The core issue in both grief and PTSD is loss, although the loss may not involve a death. Overwhelming threats in which no death occurred may result in PTSD when the events are so threatening that the experiencers lose the normal feeling of confidence that the world is safe and that they and their loved ones are not likely to be harmed. For example, the person could be in a plane that nearly crashes or witness an event in which his or her child nearly dies. Loss that results in grief with no PTSD may also not involve death. For example, the person may be in grief over losing a job or having a marriage fail.

Because this book explains induced after-death communications, the losses described here always involve a death. Since the core issues and dynamics of grief and PTSD are nearly identical when a death is involved, I present the explanations of IADCs without making further diagnostic distinctions between the two in this book. I want to be clear, however, that PTSD is a complex disorder. While IADCs resolve feelings of sadness, guilt, and anger, and reduce the negative intrusive symptoms in both PTSD and grief, IADCs have less impact on other PTSD symptoms, such as those associated with avoidance and physiological arousal. That is especially true of cases in which the PTSD is chronic and involves a number of traumas.

Therefore, although IADCs address the most painful aspects of the trauma when a death is involved, they are not appropriate for all traumas, and they do not directly address all PTSD symptoms.

The IADC Procedure
for Psychotherapists

A Note to Therapists

Although all of the steps required to complete the IADC procedure are described here, all of the necessary clinical skills that enable the therapist to be most successful with the procedure cannot be adequately conveyed in this short description. It is important for therapists to read the entire book, since some of the important clinical nuances of the procedure can be gleaned from the case material. It is not clear what success therapists will have in following this written material, and I strongly request that you give us feedback at http://induced-adc.com.

Clearly, although the steps in the IADC procedure are rather straightforward, as clinicians we are aware that each individual is complex and unique and, therefore, each step in the IADC procedure can be accomplished most successfully by a therapist who applies these steps in a manner that fits the individual psychological makeup of the patient or client.

EMDR

The following description of the IADC procedure is written in such a way that only trained EMDR therapists will be able to understand and follow the instructions. IADC therapy begins with EMDR, but applies EMDR in a manner that is markedly different from standard EMDR therapy. Most therapists using EMDR will never witness an ADC, although a few have been reported.

The IADC process begins with core-focused EMDR to directly access and process the core sadness before an IADC is attempted. You must be an EMDR-trained therapist to qualify for IADC training.

If you are not an EMDR-trained therapist, you can arrange for training by contacting the EMDR Institute:

> EMDR Institute
> P.O. Box 750
> Watsonville, CA 95077
> Telephone: (831) 761-1040
> Fax: (831) 761-1204
> Web site: http://www.emdr.com/

To be eligible for the EMDR training, you must be recognized by your state as an independent provider of mental health services.

You may read more about EMDR in the following sources:

Parnell, L. 1998. *Transforming Trauma—EMDR.* New York: WW Norton.

Shapiro, F. 2001. *Eye Movement Desensitization and Reprocessing: Basic Principles, Protocols and Procedures,* 2d ed. New York: Guilford Press.

Shapiro, F., ed. 2002. *EMDR as an Integrative Psychotherapy Approach: Experts of Diverse Orientations Explore the Paradigm Prism.* Washington, D.C.: American Psychological Association Books.

Training Workshops

The following description of the IADC procedure is derived from the training workshop handout I use when I train therapists in the techniques of IADC therapy. The procedure is explained in sufficient detail for a trained EMDR therapist to be able to induce IADCs with some success by following the explanation provided. I have found, however, that to have consistently higher percentages of IADCs, the training, demonstrations, and role-playing provided in IADC training workshops are necessary.

For more information about the IADC therapy training workshops, go to the Web page at http://induced-adc.com, or call the Center for Grief and Traumatic Loss, LLC at 847-680-0279.

A Note to Readers Who Are Not Psychotherapists

Individuals without both professional and EMDR training are unlikely to be able to induce an IADC for anyone, including themselves. The IADC method should not be attempted by anyone who does not have standard EMDR training

I compare talk therapy with EMDR therapy using this analogy. Talk therapy is like an old jalopy sputtering along the therapeutic course. It goes for a while, then breaks down with no progress. The psychotherapist tinkers with it to get it going again and it moves slowly, but breaks down again and the patient is stuck.

By contrast, EMDR, core-focused EMDR, and IADC therapy are like a Porsche that roars along the course at 200 miles per hour. It rarely slows down and at times exceeds the speeds anyone thought possible for a therapeutic method. The downside of that power is that if the patient or psychotherapist isn't able to manage the speed, the results can be harmful to the patient. It requires a highly trained professional at the wheel.

Difference from Cognitive Therapy

IADC therapy involves little cognitive processing, particularly before the IADC experience. It is not talk therapy. It is an experience. Thinking and talking are minimized because they are abstract processes that remove the patient from deep emotional processing. An experience caused the emotional problems. The patient needs to process that experience to resolve them. The processing normally occurs on a deep experiential or emotional level that usually results in a complete reversal in the underlying belief system.

Discussions after the IADC experience are normally the excitement of sharing realizations and shifts in perception that happen without guidance from the psychotherapist. Help the patient frame the experience in any way comfortable to him or her.

Importance of Allowing the IADC to Occur Naturally

You as the psychotherapist should never communicate to the patient any preconceived notions about the content of the IADC. IADCs are naturally occurring experiences that happen to people when they are in an open, receptive mode. Your receptivity, lack of expectation, and willingness to accept whatever comes are critical to the patient's successful IADC experience. If you communicate your expectations, they will probably interfere with your patient's receptive mode or block it altogether. Your expectations, even when you know the patient and the patient's case, rarely match what occurs during the IADC.

Know your own expectations and perceptions and actively work to remove them from what you say when you introduce the IADC experience to the patient and what you say during the induction.

Especially be aware that any and all senses may be involved in IADCs. At times, when a person is highly focused on one sense, such as seeing an image, that may inhibit the natural unfolding of a visual IADC. The IADC may then occur in one of the other senses: auditory, tactile, or olfactory. IADCs come in many forms. Assist the patient in normalizing his or her experience. What happens is appropriate and right for that person.

Importance of Following the Procedure

Refining the procedure over time has taught me that it does not work as effectively or may not work at all if the procedure is not followed precisely as described in this book. Since the discovery, some therapists have attempted to blend the IADC procedure with methods with which they are already comfortable, and the results have been that no IADC occurs.

My session with Juan illustrates the importance of following the procedure. At two points in this session I thought it wasn't going to work. In the first, he was feeling strong anger and I was tempted to ignore his sadness. At the second point, he was enjoying a very positive memory of his deceased daughter and it was tempting to stay with that and not move toward an IADC. At both points, however, when I returned to the basic IADC induction protocol, he was able to achieve an IADC that resulted in a more dramatic psychological shift.

About ten years before this session, Juan was arriving home from work when he saw fire engines in front of his house and flames engulfing his home. Immediately he thought of his wife and 18-month-old daughter. He jumped out of the car and ran toward the house, but a fireman stopped him. He asked about his daughter and was told that his wife had made it out, but his daughter was trapped inside the fully engulfed house. The firemen restrained him from running into the fire and the house burned to the ground.

Although the incident had happened a decade before, as Juan told me the story, he cried as though his daughter had died the day before. Time had not helped Juan at all because his daughter's death was too painful. For ten years, he had dealt with his pain through avoidance.

Juan willingly agreed to participate in an IADC procedure, but as we did the initial eye movements, he was preoccupied by intrusive thoughts of what he described as "My beautiful baby dying in a hellish inferno." He warded off the desperate grief by becoming angry at God and at the injustice of the universe. It appeared that the anger was so strong we were not going to get past it. This is the first point at which I considered truncating the session until we resolved the anger.

I knew that as long as he kept going to the anger, we would likely access other issues that angered him and he would not get to the core sadness. So I stayed with the IADC procedure and worked on the anger to decrease its intensity somewhat so we could simply bypass it. My goal wasn't for him to understand and resolve the anger. I knew that if he went into the core sadness and had the IADC, the anger would simply vanish.

I did some more eye movements to reduce the anger and the image just enough to make the core feelings of sadness more available. When the anger had reduced, I administered eye movements focusing on the sadness. The sadness increased rapidly, then began to reduce. At that point, I attempted to induce an IADC.

On the first attempt, he brought up a memory in which his daughter used to run into his arms when he got home from work. This was the second point at which I could have been tempted to abandon the IADC procedure to focus on the good memories and the positive feelings. After all, my patient was feeling better at this point. If I had, however, full resolution of his grief during an IADC would not have occurred.

I stood my ground and followed the procedure by instructing Juan not to go back to an old memory, even if it was positive. I did a set of eye movements and instructed him to close his eyes and just notice what came up.

This time he saw his daughter "smiling and happy." He said, "I can see she's still alive. She's really not dead, just in a different place." He said he was sure it wasn't a memory. From that moment, all of Juan's issues began to resolve and he felt an important reconnection with his daughter.

One week later he was able, for the first time, to tell others about the death of his daughter while maintaining emotional control. He felt that the IADC was positive because it "brought up a lot of good feelings."

Had I stopped to resolve the anger or stayed with the pleasant images Juan wanted to focus on, complete resolution would not have occurred, at least not in that session. You must follow the IADC procedure fully and precisely to induce an ADC reliably.

How Do You Know If Your Patient Had an IADC Experience?

The decision regarding whether an IADC occurred with your patient is not always as straightforward as one might think. This issue will certainly be more important to IADC researchers than to IADC clinicians. As clinicians, we are aware that the IADC experience heals regardless of beliefs, and our primary concern is healing our patients. How we categorize the patient's experience, however, is a different issue.

It would be simple if IADC experiencers could tell us whether they had the experience or not. Patient reports are very much influenced, however, by their own expectations and beliefs. I have had a few patients who believed that they had an IADC, but I thought they didn't, and I have had a few who I thought had an IADC, but they thought they didn't.

I recently had a patient who had what I thought was a series of profound IADCs with his deceased mother and father. At one point, he experienced his mother and father, who died in their eighties, looking half that age, surrounded by light, smiling, and happily dancing together. My client had an overpowering feeling that his parents were telling him they are happy and they want him to be happy too. He was surprised by his experience, sure it was not a memory. At the moment his experience unfolded, his grief appeared to resolve completely.

He had come to see me, however, with the expectation that his IADC would be much more concrete—that is, they would come in the office, sit down on chairs, and carry on an extended conversation. He was somewhat disappointed that his conversations with his parents were more private and less concrete than he had hoped. According to his own beliefs and expectations, an IADC did not occur.

I determine whether an IADC occurred or not by asking a few questions:

1. Was the content of the experience similar to other IADCs (e.g., the deceased appeared years younger or surrounded by light)?

2. Was the experience "new" in the sense that it can be differentiated from a positive memory?

3. Was the content of the experience inconsistent with expectations?

4. Was there a dramatic drop in sadness and related issues immediately following the experience that maintained over time?

If the answer is "yes" to all of the above, I would categorize the experience as an IADC. It is to be hoped that future researchers of IADC therapy will develop a more sophisticated scale for research purposes.

The Therapist Uses Words That Fit the Patient's Belief System

During sessions, speak to the patient using words that fit the patient's belief system. If the patient believes the experience to be a real communication with the deceased, talk with the patient about it using words such as "Go back and ask him . . ." or "What did she say?" If the patient does not profess such beliefs, change the instruction to fit the patient's context, saying something like "Go back to the experience."

Allow Repeated IADC Experiences to Provide the Therapy

Encourage patients to go back to the IADC and ask questions to clarify their own perceptions of the experience. I have learned, after thousands of IADCs, that the IADC always provides exactly the message the patient needs, although not necessarily what the patient wants. The messages give the patient a perspective that resolves the grief and provide answers that put to rest the patient's questions. You can be confident that the patient's own connection will guide him or her into the understanding, so you should simply induce additional experiences and allow the solutions to emerge naturally. They will come.

Potential Complications

The Varieties of Grief

Grief comes in many varieties. The most common and simplest forms of death are those of people expected to die, such as an elderly grandparent. Traumatic grief complicates the picture somewhat because survivors also experience intrusive symptoms and other symptoms suggestive of PTSD. In addition, patients may be experiencing complicated forms of grief that have been noted in the literature, such as distorted grief, chronic grief, delayed grief, and absent grief.

Regardless of the category into which your patient's grief fits, the guideline with IADC therapy is straightforward: If the patient is able to access and tolerate increases in core sadness and then enter a receptive mode, in a clear majority of cases, an IADC should occur.

Timing

You should exercise caution in pursuing the core emotions when the patient is in the initial stages of grief. Many grief authors have discussed factors typically associated with the initial stages of grief, such as denial and numbing. Denial can be positive if it provides time for the patient to gather internal and external resources to use in dealing with the loss. If the patient is in this initial stage of grieving, it might not be healthy for the patient to bare the core emotions you will uncover with core-focused EMDR. The patient may simply not be ready for it. You should use caution when the patient is in this condition.

The affective components of grief described in this book (anger, guilt, and sadness) tend to be the more chronic emotions associated with grief that can emerge at any point in the process. Grief is an individual process and your patient's individuality and individual needs come first and foremost.

Recent Losses

Experienced EMDR therapists know that the various components of a trauma event tend to consolidate in memory over time, so fewer sets of EMDR are required to process a traumatic event that occurred many years in the past. Very recent traumatic experiences are a different matter. They typically require more sets of EMDR to process the individual components, which have not yet consolidated. The same principle holds true for grief. The IADC therapist should be aware of the many components of the loss that may need to be addressed before attempting an IADC.

The Death of an Immediate Family Member

If the loss involves the death of an immediate family member, there are usually many secondary losses that affect nearly every aspect of one's life, and many of these secondary losses need to be addressed with EMDR. In these cases, as with recent losses, more sets of EMDR are generally required before an induction can be successful.

> ### A Partial List of Potential Nonconsolidated Aspects of a Recent Loss
>
> 1. The moment the news of a terminal illness, accident, or other traumatic event impacts your client
> 2. The moment the death becomes a reality
> 3. The wake
> 4. The funeral
> 5. The burial
> 6. Going through the deceased's belongings

> ### A Partial List of Secondary Losses for a Surviving Spouse—Activities That Were Once Shared with the Deceased Spouse
>
> 1. Preparing and eating meals
> 2. Going to bed/waking up
> 3. Enjoying holidays and other family activities
> 4. Managing household duties
> 5. Entertainment (e.g., dining out, visiting friends together)
> 6. Intimacy (physical, emotional)

It should also be noted that in the case of the death of an immediate family member, a complete resolution of all sadness and feelings of loss is often not possible even after a successful IADC induction. Although the

> **A Partial List of Secondary Losses for the Parents of a Deceased Child—Activities That Were Once Shared with the Deceased Child, and Anticipated Milestones That Can Now Not Be Shared**
>
> 1. Developmental and social milestones of the child (physical maturation, graduations, marriage, having children, career, and so on)
> 2. Birthdays, holidays, family activities, special events
> 3. Everyday family activities

IADC will resolve the most deep and painful feelings of sadness related to a basic sense of disconnection from the deceased, and make dealing with these secondary losses less distressing, the fact remains that the survivor has not only lost a dear loved one, but has also completely lost a way of living. Many who have lost immediate family members may require additional EMDR to cope even after a successful IADC induction. As one bereaved spouse explained to me, "I no longer feel that deep, painful sadness that I used to have, and I think I'm coping much better now, but I still feel sad when I come home from work to an empty house and have to eat dinner by myself. I know now that Bob is still with me in an important way, and I feel better knowing that, but just getting on with life is still an enormous adjustment."

Thus, especially when it comes to the recent loss of an immediate family member, more sets of EMDR are usually required both before and after an IADC. Bereaved spouses, or parents of a deceased child, are not only severely distressed by their deep sadness and sense of disconnection from their loved one, they also have sadness associated with a number of non-consolidated aspects of the loss, as well as sadness associated with a number of secondary losses.

Do EMDR and IADC Treatment Outcomes Hold Up Over Time?

Although the current research on EMDR is somewhat unclear on this issue, I am convinced that EMDR outcomes do hold up over time, as long as the core affective issue (either sadness or fear—the only two primary/core emotions) is sufficiently processed. If the EMDR therapist processes and reduces only the peripheral/defensive emotions, the patient may report some relief, but the positive outcome will be only temporary. The core emotion must be successfully processed for the outcome to hold up over time.

Although clinical experience indicates that IADC outcomes hold up extremely well over time, there have been a few cases in which patients reported that their sadness returned. In these cases, however, I found that their sadness returned because something else "pulled" it back. In each case, the therapist should ignore what was previously treated, and directly treat what is doing the pulling. In every case, once I eliminated what was doing the pulling, the original issue did not require any further attention.

The following are the most likely "pullers."

1. **Depression:** When patients become clinically depressed, their thinking, of course, puts a negative slant on everything. An increase in depression can "pull" back their sadness over a previously treated loss. In these cases, the issue is depression, not the reemergence of grief. The IADC therapist will find that treating the depression (sometimes just a good antidepressant) is all that is needed to return the previous positive IADC outcome to its original level.

2. **Current or recent life experiences:** Although our emotional responses to all ongoing events are clearly shaped by our prior emotional experiences, it is also true that our emotional response to memories of past events is influenced by our current emotions. Some patients, for example, report that their sadness returned over a loss previously treated with IADC therapy after they experienced another more recent loss. In these cases, treating the more recent loss is all that is needed for the previous positive IADC outcome to return to its original level.

3. **Untreated nonconsolidated and secondary components of grief:** As noted in the section on potential complications in IADC therapy, a recent loss, or the loss of an immediate family member generally requires more sets of EMDR to address the various components of the loss. Any component that was not previously processed with EMDR can "pull" the sadness associated with aspects of the loss that were

successfully processed. In these cases, treating these additional components is all that is needed for the previous positive IADC outcome to return to its original level.

The IADC Procedure

The IADC discovery occurred only after I made a number of significant changes to standard EMDR. These must be followed to successfully perform IADCs with a high degree of reliability.

I. Screen/History

A) Screen for a history of other traumas or losses that may emerge during the therapy.

B) Inquire about medications.

1. Those that blunt effect (most antianxiety and antipsychotic medications) can interfere.

2. Antidepressants are OK. Depression can interfere with progress in any form of psychotherapy.

C) Assess suicide potential (as you would with all patients).

D) Assess support systems (family, friends, and so on).

II. Core-Focused EMDR

A) Stay with one grief issue or trauma (vs. following a patient's associations).

1. I found that following a patient's associations and thereby uncovering numerous traumas without fully processing any one appeared to provide dubious progress, and it left patients feeling worse.

2. The only thing more powerful than EMDR is resistance (the patient's desire to avoid pain).

3. I therefore instructed patients to stay with one trauma and found that patients more often left the sessions feeling better, with an increased confidence in EMDR and increased sense of self-efficacy.

B) Rank traumas according to the degree of distress each causes the patient and begin with the most distressing (vs. working on the trauma the patient chooses to address).

1. While I found that focusing on one trauma at a time greatly improved psychotherapeutic outcomes, exceptions occurred when patients addressed a

memory with EMDR that was less distressing than a different trauma/memory. In these cases, the more distressing memory was inadvertently uncovered/accessed.

2. EMDR accomplishes two psychotherapeutic goals better than any other treatment: uncovering/accessing and desensitization. EMDR tends to uncover the patient's most emotionally charged memory, however, and not necessarily the one the patient chooses or is ready to address.

3. Therefore, before I begin EMDR, I take some time to help the patient rank his/her memories, and we begin with the most distressing memory first. This eliminated the problem noted in B1.

C) Instruct patients to close their eyes (vs. keep their eyes open) after each EMDR set.

1. I found over the years that patients who spontaneously closed their eyes after each set of EMDR achieved better results from each set.

2. It appears that accelerated processing continues for a brief time after each set of EMDR.

3. I, therefore, began to instruct all patients to close their eyes after each set, and results improved.

D) Address core sadness.

1. I have found that feelings associated with a trauma and grief come in layers. Anger/numbing and guilt serve to protect one from sadness and are, therefore, secondary or peripheral to core sadness.

2. I, therefore, begin each session by directly addressing sadness with EMDR, and ignoring the peripheral emotions. I have found that, in nearly all cases, the anger and guilt vanish without being directly addressed, or if they need to be addressed after the sadness has been processed, it is usually a rather quick and easy task (i.e., one or two additional sets).

III. The Induction

A) Prepare the patient by giving a full explanation of the procedure.

B) Have the client tell his/her story (e.g., relationship issues, circumstances of death).

C) For simple (nontraumatic) grief, first warn the patient that his/her sadness is likely to increase dramatically at first. Then begin EMDR on the sadness. If it goes up, immediately provide another set of EMDR.

D) For a traumatic loss, provide EMDR on intrusive aspects of the loss, and then address the sadness.

E) It is not necessary to fully reduce sadness and attendant intrusive symptoms before beginning the IADC, but it is essential that sadness and intrusions have begun to decrease in intensity.

F) Ask patients what they would say to the deceased if they could talk to him or her (frame the question in a way consistent with the patient's belief system). A number of different statements can be made prior to the actual induction of receptivity. I like this one because it alerts the therapist to the primary issues. Never suggest the content of the experience in any way. Take time to help the patient fully develop what he or she wants to say, so that all of the patient's main issues are verbalized.

G) Then remind the patient about the receptive mode, and instruct the patient to "just go with whatever happens," or "let the experience come to you." This should be repeated with each subsequent induction.

H) Tell the patient that IADCs usually occur soon after EMDR is provided, and therefore, he/she should open his/her eyes after 15 seconds or so if nothing happens.

I) When the patient opens his/her eyes, ask what happened. If no IADC occurred, it is usually because not all intrusions were decreased or the patient was trying to make the IADC happen. For intrusions, apply EMDR; for trying, simply remind the patient not to try and to "just let it happen." (The patient may also need a set of EMDR to further relax.) If the client says nothing happened, ask what he/she means. It is rare for people to close their eyes and have absolutely nothing happen. They will at least have random thoughts and images pass through their consciousness, and these experiences may be interfering with the receptive mode. Sometimes an IADC experience may start with colors, a pinpoint of light, or some other subtle sensory impression. Encourage the patient: "Good, you're doing a good job."

J) If the patient has an IADC, evaluate whether all issues the patient brought to the experience are resolved. If not, have the patient hold in mind whatever issue remains and induce the patient again. Repeat until all issues are resolved.

K) IADCs can be visual, auditory, tactile, or olfactory, and most often involve a combination of these sensory modalities. Normalize your patient's experience (i.e., most people characteristically experience IADCs in the same sensory modes from one experience to another). Also, if the patient is trying too hard in one modality, the experience often comes through a different modality in which he or she is more receptive.

L) Take some time to assist patients in framing the experience in any way that is comfortable for them.

IV. Follow-up Session

A) As with any EMDR, one must make sure that no other distressing issues surfaced since the last EMDR session.

B) Explore with the patient both the positive and negative aftereffects of the prior session. Provide EMDR or IADC for any negative issues that remain.

C) Once a patient has had one successful IADC, the chances of doing another are nearly 100 percent; therefore, the patient may want to do more.

V. Other Observations

A) If patients find themselves going in a tunnel during their IADC, it is usually because they are trying too hard (follow previous instructions).

B) It is not necessary for the patient to have had a close personal relationship with the deceased, but the personal connection needs to be significant (e.g., observing the death of a stranger, killing another in an accident).

C) IADCs can occur with groups of deceased if the group is related in some way (e.g., family, combat squad members).

D) Sometimes the deceased forgive survivors, and sometimes survivors forgive the deceased. Regardless of the nature of the relationship between the survivor and the deceased, so far, in my experience and that of my colleagues, all interpersonal problems (unfinished business) have resolved with an IADC.

E) All IADCs are positive unless misinterpreted by the experiencer. If the patient reports a negative IADC, instruct the patient to go back and clarify the message/experience.

F) Many therapists attempt to blend the IADC procedure with methods with which they are already comfortable. In my experience, those who do such blending report a reduced percentage of IADC successes. It is important to follow the IADC protocol exactly.

G) Check your own beliefs and enthusiasm as a therapist. Again, IADCs are naturally occurring experiences that happen to people when they are in an open, receptive mode and not expecting it. If your expectations, no matter how enlightened, are communicated to your patient, they will interfere with your patient's receptive mode. Any expectations on the part of your patient will block the experience, whether they originate from your patient or you. Remember that IADCs come as a surprise to people, no matter how enlightened they are.

H) If the client appears stuck while receiving EMDR, in my experience the chances are about 90 percent that the client has accessed a different issue. Ask the patient if any other issues are coming up. If the intruding issue is more distresssing, it may need to be addressed first.

What I Learned from the First 84 Cases

I wanted to draw generalizations from my first cases to help me understand the phenomenon, so I analyzed the first 84 patients to whom I offered an IADC induction. My analysis follows. Although an overwhelming majority of these patients chose to do an additional IADC after their initial one, only first attempts are represented here. In general, IADCs become easier to induce with additional successes. A table summarizing the results of these first 84 cases follows.

Summary of the Results of the First 84 IADC Cases

Cases in which an IADC induction was offered	84
Number of cases willing to participate in the induction	83
Percentage that achieved an IADC	81/83 (98%)
Percentage of IADCs that provided full resolution of core sadness	78/81 (96%)
Percentage that believed their IADC was spiritual (an actual contact with the deceased)	76/81 (94%)
Of those who believed their IADC was actual contact, the percentage that believed prior to the IADC that actual contact was possible by induction	6/76 (8%)

It is clear that patients are very willing to attempt an induction for the first time, even though they generally believe beforehand that such an experience is not possible. This, of course, depends on the trust the patient has in the therapist to try something different, something that might even sound a little crazy at first. If the patient is then willing and able to participate in the procedure, an IADC should reliably occur.

People who experience IADCs, in a vast majority of cases, believe that their experience was actual contact with the deceased. This was the only information I recorded on a regular basis, other than the verbal reports of my patients. Although I initially had some interest in the potential effects of varying prior belief systems on IADC outcomes, I never kept a record of that data. I worked with many patients, however, who professed atheism, many who were uncertain about religious beliefs, and many who professed strong religious or spiritual beliefs.

The fact that 98 percent of subjects achieve IADCs strongly suggests that prior beliefs play no role in the production of the experience.

Bibliography

Botkin, A. 2000. The induction of after-death communications utilizing eye movement desensitization and reprocessing: A new discovery. *Journal of Near-Death Studies* 18(3), 181–209.

Cardeña, E., Lynn, S. J., and Krippner, S., eds. 2000. *Varieties of Anomalous Experience: Examining the Scientific Evidence.* Washington, D.C.: American Psychological Association.

Deits, B. 2000. *Life after Loss: A Personal Guide Dealing with Death, Divorce, Job Change, and Relocation,* 3d ed. Tucson, Ariz.: Fisher Books.

Eves, H. W., comp. 1977. *Mathematical Circles Adieu: A Fourth Collection of Mathematical Stories and Anecdotes.* Boston: Prindle, Weber and Schmidt.

Guggenheim, B., and Guggenheim, J. 1995. *Hello from Heaven!* New York: Bantam.

Klass, D., Silverman, P., and Nickman, S. 1996. *Continuing Bonds: New Understandings of Grief.* London: Taylor and Francis.

Levin, P., Lazgrove, S., and van der Kolk, B. A. 1999. What psychological testing and neuroimaging tell us about the treatment of posttraumatic stress disorder (PTSD) by eye movement desensitization and reprocessing (EMDR). *Journal of Anxiety Disorders* 13, 159–172.

Lipke, H., and Botkin, A. 1992. Case studies of eye movement desensitization and reprocessing (EMDR) with chronic post-traumatic stress disorder. *Psychotherapy* 29(4), 591–595.

Moody, R. 1985. *Reflections on Life after Life.* New York: Bantam.

———. 1993. *Reunions: Visionary Encounters with Departed Love Ones.* New York: Villard.

———. 1999. *The Last Laugh.* Charlottesville, Va.: Hampton Roads.

———. 2001. *Life after Life.* San Francisco, Calif.: HarperSanFrancisco.

Mossbridge, J. 2003. Grief relief: Visiting the dead. *Conscious Choice* (November 2003).

Parnell, L. 1998. *Transforming Trauma—EMDR.* New York: WW Norton.

Shapiro, F. 2001. *Eye Movement Desensitization and Reprocessing: Basic Principles, Protocols and Procedures,* 2d ed. New York: Guilford Press.

Shapiro, F., ed. 2002. *EMDR as an Integrative Psychotherapy Approach: Experts of Diverse Orientations Explore the Paradigm Prism.* Washington, D.C.: American Psychological Association Books.

Index

About the Authors

Allan Botkin received his Doctor of Psychology degree from Baylor University in 1983. for the next 20 years he worked in private practice and as a staff psychologist for the Department of Veterans Affairs in the Chicago area. His specialty is the diagnosis and treatment of post-traumatic stress disorder (PTSD). Br. Botkin has treated combat veterans from WWII, the Korean War, the Vietnam War, and Desert Storm. He has also published scientific papers in the areas of brain function, PTSD, and eye-movement desensitization and reprocessing (EMDR). He is currently the director of the Center for Grief and Traumatic Loss, LLC in Libertyville, Illinois. For more information on IADC therapy and training go to www.inducedadc.com, or call the center at 847-680-0279.

R. Craig Hogan, Ph.D., is owner and director of the Business Writing Center, an online school that trains business writers around the world (http://writingtrainers.com). He is the author of *Explicit Business Writing*, a book describing today's best practices in business writing (available at http://bwcpublications.com). He has been the interpersonal development coordinator at a graduate school where he taught interpersonal growth courses, administrator at two universities and a medical school, and professor of communications at three universities. He co-authored a book for school administrators, teaching them how to work more cooperatively and productively with teachers, and is co-author of the *Personal Styles Inventory* (3rd edition, Organization Design and Development, 2005) based on Carl Jung's work. You can reach him at r.craig.hogan@inducedadc.com or 800-690-4232.

Hampton Roads Publishing Company

. . . for the evolving human spirit

HAMPTON ROADS PUBLISHING COMPANY publishes books on a variety of subjects, including metaphysics, spirituality, health, visionary fiction, and other related topics.

We also create on-line courses and sponsor an *Applied Learning Series* of author workshops. For a current list of what is available, go to www.hrpub.com, or request the ALS workshop catalog at our toll-free number.

For a copy of our latest trade catalog, call toll-free, 800-766-8009, or send your name and address to:

HAMPTON ROADS PUBLISHING COMPANY, INC.
1125 STONEY RIDGE ROAD • CHARLOTTESVILLE, VA 22902
e-mail: hrpc@hrpub.com • www.hrpub.com